Please note: All oven temperatures are for a fan forced oven unless otherwise stated.

Good Food Favourite Recipes
Edited by Ardyn Bernoth
First published in Australia in 2019 by
Simon & Schuster (Australia) Pty Limited
Suite 19A, Level 1, Building C, 450 Miller Street, Cammeray, NSW 2062

10 9 8 7 6 5 4 3 2 1

A CBS Company
Sydney New York London Toronto New Delhi
Visit our website at www.simonandschuster.com.au

 A catalogue record for this
book is available from the
National Library of Australia

Publishing Director, Good Food: Trudi Jenkins
Life Editor: Monique Farmer
Life Executive Assistant: Caroline Hartnett
Publisher for Simon & Schuster: Julie Gibbs
Text editor: Pru Engel
Index: Fay Donlevy
Cover image photography: William Meppem
Cover image styling: Hannah Meppem
Internal food styling: Hannah Meppem, except Katrina Meynink's images styled by her
Cover, internal design and typesetting: Daniel New
Printed by Asia Pacific Offset

The paper used to produce this book is a natural, recyclable product made from wood
grown in sustainable plantation forests. The manufacturing processes conform to the
environmental regulations in the country of origin.

ISBN 9781760851408

goodfood

Danielle Alvarez
Jill Dupleix
Helen Goh
Kylie Kwong
Dan Lepard
Adam Liaw
Andrew McConnell
Katrina Meynink
Neil Perry

Favourite Recipes

Edited by Ardyn Bernoth

SIMON &
SCHUSTER

London · New York · Sydney · Toronto · New Delhi
A CBS COMPANY

Contents

Welcome

When we asked Neil Perry for a biography of his career in 80 words to feature in this book, he jokingly replied that he might have to ignore the first 30 years and just focus on the last 10.

He was right. This man – one of Australia's most influential chefs – has owned and operated more than 15 award-winning restaurants, penned more than ten cookbooks, and currently leads the Rockpool Dining Group while clocking up 20 years as a Creative Director at Qantas.

Perry is one of nine recipe columnists we are incredibly proud to work with at Good Food. Between them they have careers that involve filming television series, writing a library full of cookbooks, running hatted restaurants, editing restaurant guides and generally being at the top of the food industry game.

There is the inimitable Kylie Kwong who has given the world a new cooking style, native Australian Chinese food. Helen Goh, who works alongside Yotam Ottolenghi in London, and Andrew McConnell, one of Melbourne's most influential and awarded restaurateurs.

Week after week they, along with other food legends Jill Dupleix, Danielle Alvarez, Dan Lepard, Adam Liaw and Katrina Meynink, file their beautiful recipes to us which we publish on Tuesday in Good Food and on Saturday in *Good Weekend*.

Our brief to these leading chefs is simple: give us the food you are passionate about which reflects the seasons but make it approachable. People who cook these recipes – you, our readers – are not professional chefs. We need recipes for weeknight meals that can be made after a tough day at work, in between ballet and footy pickups, as much as we need the show-stopping numbers like Danielle Alvarez's chocolate, coconut butterscotch and raspberry trifle (see page 207).

What I love about working with these consummate professionals is that they have an eye on the latest trends in food and cooking while being grounded in the best training and technique. Which means we are, too.

To save you a pile of dog-eared, newsprint articles, we have collated over 100 of their recipes from the last two years in this book. You will find an emphasis on cooking with vegetables, as current trends dictate, along with beautiful meat and seafood dishes, finishing with the most decadent desserts.

These recipes will bring you, your friends and family around a table sharing the delicious joy of Good Food.

Ardyn Bernoth
National editor, Good Food

About the authors

Danielle Alvarez champions a produce-driven philosophy at one of Sydney's most-loved restaurants, Fred's. An alumnus of Napa Valley's three-Michelin-starred French Laundry and former mentee of Alice Waters at Chez Panisse, Danielle has puts her passion for sustainability into action at Fred's, carefully curating a list of local farmers who provide the bulk of the restaurant's ethically produced and all-natural fare.

Jill Dupleix is a long-time Good Food recipe columnist, restaurant critic and author of 16 cookbooks. The former food editor for *The Times* in London, she is currently food editor of *The Australian Financial Review Magazine*, and founding editor of *Truth, Love & Clean Cutlery* – the world's first guide to sustainable and ethical dining.

Malaysian born and Australian-bred, **Helen Goh** defected from a career in psychology to hone her skills in her true love, cooking, at a number of Melbourne restaurants. After moving to the UK, she became part of the Ottolenghi creative team. Her first book with Yotam, *Sweet*, was published in 2017 and, while working on her second book, she writes a weekly baking column in *Good Weekend*.

Kylie Kwong, chef and restaurateur, has become synonymous with Chinese cooking in Australia through her unique combination of Australian native ingredients with traditional Cantonese cuisine. Her advocacy of sustainability and collaboration extends to her involvement with community organisations including The Wayside Chapel and René Redzepi's MAD Mondays Sydney.

Dan Lepard, best known for his innovative baking and vegetable-rich recipes, is based in London but travels the world as the culinary whizz top chefs like Yotam Ottolenghi and Giorgio Locatelli call in to advise on their menus. Author of the sourdough bible *The Handmade Loaf,* he's the chef to guide you through the complexities of fermentation, rare grains and curious flours as well as getting straight down to sorting out a mega family dinner that's quick and easy.

Adam Liaw understands how Australian families eat. As the author of six cookbooks and host of the award-winning SBS television series *Destination Flavour*, his approachable and family-friendly recipes are influenced by his global travels, but remain focussed on the casual simplicity of contemporary Australian home cooking. In 2016 the Japanese government appointed Adam as an official Goodwill Ambassador for Japanese Cuisine.

Chef/restaurateur **Andrew McConnell** defines Melbourne's culinary landscape. His restaurants collectively reflect how Melburnians like to eat, celebrating the flavours and seasonality of Victoria. With two of his restaurants now over a decade old, Cumulus Inc. and the award-winning Cutler & Co, Andrew's influence has positioned Melbourne as a world-class culinary destination.

Food writer and recipe developer, **Katrina Meynink** has published two cookbooks, *Kitchen Coquette* and *Bistronomy French Food Unbound*, and a picture book *Lulu Le Baby Chef*. She contributes recipes to a number of publications and draws on her background in journalism and gastronomy related education to assist chefs in developing and writing cookbooks. She has received several scholarships through the James Beard Foundation and Le Cordon Bleu.

Neil Perry AM is one of Australia's leading, most influential chefs. He has owned and operated many award-winning restaurants, and today leads the Rockpool Dining Group culinary team as Chief Brand & Culinary Officer. Neil also recently celebrated 20 years as Creative Director, Food, Beverage & Service at Qantas.

Soups

Mussel, fennel and chorizo soup **12**

Chicken, chilli and Hokkien noodle soup **14**

Pumpkin miso ramen **17**

Rustic seafood and potato soup with chorizo jam **18**

Tomato, prawn and lemongrass laksa **20**

Cream of fennel and parmesan soup **22**

Garlic, sweet potato and chickpea soup **23**

Roasted leek, potato and bacon soup with caramelised balsamic prosciutto **24**

Green pea and spinach soup with burnt butter **26**

Mussel, fennel and chorizo soup

Easy
🕐 **less than 30 mins**
Serves 4

1kg mussels, cleaned and
    debearded
2 tbsp extra virgin olive oil
120g chorizo sausage, sliced
1 small red onion, finely diced
4 cloves garlic, thinly sliced
1 tsp sea salt
1 baby fennel bulb, diced
2 tsp smoked sweet paprika
1 tsp of mild chilli flakes
250ml dry sherry
2 tbsp tomato paste
400g can chopped tomatoes
500ml chicken stock
4 tbsp unsalted butter
1 lemon, juiced, plus lemon
    cheeks, to serve
freshly ground black pepper
2 tbsp flat-leaf parsley leaves,
    roughly chopped
crusty bread, to serve

I love the salty sea flavour of mussels, which comes from the juice encased in their shells. This dish is perfect with a garlic-rubbed piece of bread drizzled with olive oil. But you could make it even more hearty by folding cooked pasta through the finished dish. Equally I love it served with rice, with a leafy green side salad and a good glass of riesling.

1. Place mussels in a large pot over high heat, cover with a tight-fitting lid and cook for 3-5 minutes until the mussels start to open. Check and remove the open mussels with tongs and place into a bowl. Continue to check and remove mussels until they are all open. Reserve the remaining mussel juice and strain through a fine sieve to remove grit. When cool, take the mussels out of their shells.

2. Heat the olive oil in a large heavy-based saucepan over medium heat, add the chorizo and fry until golden brown.

3. Add onion, garlic and sea salt to the pan and cook until the onion starts to soften. Add fennel, paprika and chilli and continue cooking until the fennel softens.

4. Add sherry and simmer until the liquid has reduced by half. Add tomato paste, stir well and simmer for 5 minutes, then pour in tomatoes, stock and the reserved mussel juice. Bring to the boil, then reduce heat and simmer for 5 minutes.

5. Fold the mussels back into the soup and heat through, add the butter, lemon juice, a good grind of pepper and the parsley. Divide between 4 soup bowls and serve with lemon cheeks and crusty bread.

Soups

Chicken, chilli and Hokkien noodle soup

Easy
Dairy-free
🕐 **less than 30 mins**
Serves 4

½ bunch (about 200g) bok choy
450g pre-cooked Hokkien noodles
6 cups rich homemade Chinese
  chicken stock
3 tbsp light soy sauce
1 tbsp ginger, cut into matchsticks
1 tsp white sugar
400g free-range chicken thigh fillet,
  cut widthways into 1cm slices
1 tsp sesame oil
½ cup spring onions, cut into
  matchsticks
2 large red chillies, finely sliced on
  the diagonal

*A homemade stock is best but you
  can substitute with store-bought
  chicken stock if necessary.

You can use any type of noodles in this soup, including fresh rice noodles, thin egg noodles and Shanghai noodles. If you are using vacuum-packed, pre-cooked noodles, rinse them under hot running water to untangle them and drain before adding to the soup. I prefer to use fresh Hokkien noodles, available at Asian grocers. Prepare them as you would fresh pasta, blanching them in a pot of boiling salted water and draining before adding to your soup.

1. Remove cores from bok choy, cut crossways into four, then wash thoroughly and drain.

2. Place noodles in a colander and rinse well under hot running water, then drain.

3. Bring stock to the boil in a large heavy-based pot. Add soy sauce, ginger and sugar and stir to combine.

4. Reduce heat, add drained noodles, and simmer gently for 30 seconds. Add bok choy and chicken and simmer for a further 2 minutes or until chicken is cooked through. Stir in sesame oil, then remove pot from heat.

5. Ladle soup into large bowls. Place spring onion and chilli in a separate bowl and serve alongside the soup.

goodfood

Pumpkin miso ramen

Easy
Vegan
🕑 **30 mins–1 hour**
Serves 4

Pumpkin
600g pumpkin, cut into
   large chunks
1 tbsp white miso
1 tsp soy sauce
1 tbsp rice bran oil (or other
   flavourless oil)
1 heaped tsp brown sugar

Broth
3½ cups vegetable stock
10cm piece ginger, peeled
   and sliced
2 cloves garlic, crushed
1 spring onion, finely chopped
100g ramen noodles
¼ cup white miso paste
1 tbsp soy sauce

To serve
1 bunch broccolini
1 bok choy
kernels from 2 cobs corn
coriander leaves, sesame seeds
   and finely sliced nori (optional)

If you would prefer a chilled broth, you can place it in the fridge for at least an hour or until completely chilled before pouring into serving bowls. Then just steam the greens before plating and serving.

1. **For the pumpkin**, preheat oven to 180°C. Add the pumpkin ingredients to a bowl and toss until the pieces are coated, then spread on a large baking tray lined with baking paper. Roast for 30 minutes or until the pumpkin is cooked through and caramelised on the edges.

2. Meanwhile, prepare the broth. Pour stock into a saucepan over medium heat, add the ginger, garlic and spring onion and bring to a simmer. Cook for 20 minutes to allow the flavours to infuse. Reduce heat to low, add noodles and cook until tender (about 3 minutes – follow packet instructions for further guidance).

3. Remove pan from heat and stir the miso paste and soy sauce into the broth. Taste the broth and dilute with boiling water if you want a more subtle flavour. Gently remove the noodles and strain the broth into a large bowl.

4. To serve, pour the hot broth into serving bowls and place broccolini, bok choy and corn directly into the broth so they cook in the residual heat. Add reserved noodles and roasted pumpkin pieces and top with coriander leaves, sesame seeds and finely sliced nori, if using.

Rustic seafood and potato soup with chorizo jam

Make the chorizo jam ahead of time and use leftovers on eggs, steak or smashed avo toast.

Gluten-free
🕒 **30 mins–1 hour**
Serves 4

Chorizo jam

2 chorizo sausages (about 200g), casing removed, meat roughly chopped*
2 red onions, peeled and sliced
⅓ cup brown sugar
⅓ cup red wine vinegar

Soup

4-6 new potatoes, scrubbed and quartered
1½ tbsp olive oil
4 shallots, peeled and finely diced
3 cloves garlic, peeled and crushed
¼ fennel bulb, washed, trimmed and finely sliced
1 celery stalk, washed, trimmed and finely chopped
1 tbsp ras el hanout
3 small roma tomatoes, quartered
10 saffron threads
4 slices of preserved lemon, finely chopped
1½ cups chicken stock
1 cup white wine
300ml cream
2 cups mixed seafood (such as raw prawns, scallops and white fish – you may need to vary cooking times depending on the seafood chosen)

*Check the chorizo is gluten-free, if required.

1 **For the chorizo jam,** add chorizo and onion to a small frying pan over low-medium heat and cook for 15 minutes or until the meat is cooked and the onion has softened. Add the brown sugar and red wine vinegar and cook for 10 minutes. Allow to cool, place in a blender and briefly pulse until blended but still chunky. Set aside until ready to serve.

2 **For the soup,** add potatoes, olive oil, shallot, garlic, fennel and celery to a large saucepan over medium heat. Cook, stirring regularly, for about 15 minutes or until the onions are softened and the mixture is fragrant.

3. Add ras el hanout and cook for 30 seconds then add tomato. Cook for 1–2 minutes until the tomatoes release their juices, then add the saffron, preserved lemon, stock and white wine. Simmer for 10 minutes then add the cream and simmer for an additional 15 minutes or until the soup has reduced slightly and thickened.

4. Add the seafood and cook for 1–2 minutes or until just cooked through, before adding soup to serving bowls. Top with dollops of chorizo jam and serve immediately.

Tomato, prawn and lemongrass laksa

Easy
Dairy-free
🕐 **less than 30 mins**
Serves 4

1 tbsp vegetable oil

2 stalks lemongrass, white part
only, bruised

5cm piece ginger, peeled and
thinly sliced

3 cloves garlic, crushed

2 tbsp laksa paste

¼ cup Asian chilli jam, plus an
extra 1 tbsp

400g can crushed tomatoes

1 litre vegetable or chicken stock

1½ tbsp fish sauce (or to taste)

juice and zest of 1 lime

16 green prawns, peeled,
tails intact

250g flat rice noodles

Asian herbs, bean sprouts, sliced
red chilli and fresh lime, to serve

Borrowing from tom yum, this fragrant tomato-based soup is refreshing with just the right amount of heat, flavour and crunch, but without the heaviness of a coconut milk base.

1. Heat oil in a large saucepan over high heat. Add lemongrass, ginger and garlic and cook, stirring often, for 2 minutes or until fragrant. Add laksa paste and cook until it starts to separate then add chilli jam, tomatoes and stock. Bring to the boil and simmer for 20 minutes. Add fish sauce and lime juice to taste.

2. While the laksa is cooking, place a non-stick frying pan over high heat. Add prawns and cook for 2 minutes, turning often or until just browning. Quickly add the extra chilli jam and cook for a further 20 seconds or until prawns darken and char slightly. Cook the noodles according to packet instructions, strain and divide among serving bowls.

3. Discard the lemongrass stalks from the laksa broth. Place 4 cooked prawns in each serving bowl and pour over enough soup to cover. Serve piping hot with additional toppings of your choice.

goodfood

Cream of fennel and parmesan soup

Easy

🕐 **30 mins–1 hour**

Serves 4

2 tbsp extra virgin olive oil,
  plus extra to serve
2 medium fennel bulbs, cut into
  2cm pieces
6 cloves garlic, finely chopped
sea salt
1½ litres chicken stock
3 handfuls of fresh basil leaves,
  plus extra to garnish
125ml pure cream
40g grated parmesan, plus extra
  to serve
freshly ground pepper

This soup is perfect as a starter, but hearty enough to be a great lunch or supper. To make it a main course, serve in a big bowl with slices of good-quality toasted sourdough, rubbed with garlic and drizzled with olive oil.

1. Heat oil in a heavy-based saucepan over medium heat, then add the fennel, garlic and a good pinch of sea salt. Cook for about 10 minutes, stirring occasionally, or until the fennel starts to soften.

2. Add stock, bring to the boil, then reduce the heat to low and simmer, uncovered, for about 20 minutes. Add the basil and cook for a further 2 minutes.

3. Pour the soup into a blender and pulse until well pureed but not completely smooth – you want the soup to have a bit of texture. Return to the pan and stir in the cream and parmesan.

4. Divide the soup among bowls, add a good grind of black pepper and drizzle with olive oil. Sprinkle with extra basil leaves and grated parmesan to serve.

DAN LEPARD

Garlic, sweet potato and chickpea soup

Easy
Vegan
🕐 **less than 30 mins**
Serves 4–6

A super-comforting, ward-away-the-blues autumnal soup with a rich sweet flavour that's offset by a squeeze of lemon and a few twists of ground black pepper added to soup bowls at the table.

8 large cloves garlic, peeled and sliced
1 onion, peeled and chopped
30g olive oil
350g cooked sweet potato
400g can chickpeas, drained
800ml water
1 tsp salt
2 tsp dried thyme
2 tsp ground turmeric, or 3cm piece fresh turmeric, peeled and grated
½ tsp ground cayenne pepper
lemon juice and black pepper to serve

1. Place garlic, onion, olive oil and a splash of water in a large saucepan over medium heat: the water creates extra steam to soften the garlic quickly. Bring to the boil then reduce the heat and cook for 5 minutes until the water has evaporated and garlic is very soft.

2. Add sweet potato, chickpeas, water, salt, thyme, turmeric and cayenne then bring to the boil, cooking until the sweet potato has softened further. Remove from heat and leave to cool slightly.

3. Puree mixture in a blender until smooth. Return to the pan, adjust the consistency with extra water if needed, then bring to the boil. Divide among 4–6 bowls and add a drizzle of lemon juice and a couple of grinds of black pepper to serve.

KATRINA MEYNINK

Roasted leek, potato and bacon soup with caramelised balsamic prosciutto

Yes. OK. The world hardly needs another potato soup recipe but the double-down of bacon and prosciutto with a hint of white wine is definitely worth adding to your rotation.

🕐 **1–2 hours**
Serves 4–6

4 leeks, white part only, washed and halved lengthways
1½ tbsp olive oil
200g smoked bacon, roughly chopped
800g floury potatoes, peeled and chopped into 5cm chunks
500ml chicken stock
1 tbsp balsamic vinegar
1 tbsp brown sugar
12 slices prosciutto
1 cup white wine
300ml cream
2 spring onions, finely sliced
freshly ground black pepper, to serve

*Check cured meats are gluten-free, if required

1. Preheat oven to 185°C. Place leeks and oil in a roasting tray and toss to coat. Roast the leeks for 30–45 minutes or until they are soft and lightly charred at the edges.

2. Meanwhile, fry off the bacon in a small frying pan until crisp. Set aside to cool.

3. Allow the roasted leek halves to cool before adding to a saucepan with the potatoes, bacon and chicken stock. Season to taste, bring to a simmer, cover and cook for 20–25 minutes or until potato breaks down and soup thickens.

4. While the soup is simmering, add the balsamic vinegar and brown sugar to a small bowl and stir until sugar dissolves. Place the prosciutto slices on a baking tray lined with baking paper and drizzle over the balsamic mixture. Roast in the oven for 10 minutes or until crisp, and the balsamic mixture has caramelised.

5. Once the soup has thickened, add white wine and cook for a further 5 minutes. Turn off the heat and stir through the cream. Blend the soup using a hand-held blender (or in a food processor in batches) until mostly smooth – some texture of the bacon should remain. Season generously to taste.

6. Pour soup into bowls, and top each with a few slices of crisp prosciutto and spring onion, and sprinkle with pepper, to serve.

Green pea and spinach soup with burnt butter

Easy
🕐 **less than 30 mins**
Serves 4

60g butter
1 small brown onion, peeled
    and diced
280g baby spinach leaves
2 cups frozen peas
3 cups chicken stock or
    vegetable stock
salt and pepper, to season

Is there anything more wholesome than a green soup?
This one is bursting with good stuff and is glammed up
with a decadent burnt butter sauce. Break out the blender!

1. Heat half the butter in a medium saucepan over medium heat,
   add onion and cook for about 3 minutes or until fragrant and
   translucent. Add spinach and peas and cook for about 5 minutes,
   stirring, until the spinach has wilted. You can add a little of the
   stock during this process if the pan is too dry.

2. Add the stock and reduce heat to a simmer. Season with salt.
   Simmer for about 5 minutes, then remove from the heat. Allow to
   cool for a minute or two, then transfer to a blender. Carefully blend
   the mixture (see tip, below) until smooth.

3. Taste and adjust the seasoning if necessary. Divide the soup
   between bowls. Heat remaining butter in a small pan over medium
   heat until it turns medium brown and has a nutty aroma (about
   4 minutes). Drizzle about a teaspoon over each bowl and add
   a grind of black pepper to serve

◆ **Tip** When mixing hot liquids in a blender, don't allow pressure to build up
   in the container. Cover it with a lid but be sure to leave the centre cap open.
   Start at a very slow speed and increase it gradually.

Carrot and sultana salad

Easy
Vegan
🕐 **less than 30 mins**
Serves 4

250g large carrots, peeled,
  trimmed, julienned
1 tbsp caster sugar
1 cinnamon stick
pinch of salt
2 tbsp fresh lemon juice
75g sultanas
1 tbsp orange flower water
3 tbsp extra virgin olive oil
1 tbsp orange juice
sea salt
freshly ground pepper
handful coriander, to garnish

The crispness of fresh carrot paired with the sweetness of sultanas is marvellous. This is a simple and bright salad recipe that will be memorable.

1. Place carrots in a small saucepan and add the sugar, cinnamon stick, salt and lemon juice, then cover with water.

2. Bring to the boil, then reduce to a simmer and cook for about 5 minutes or until tender. Drain the carrots in a sieve set over a bowl and use the hot liquid to soak the sultanas.

3. Once they've cooled, drain sultanas and mix with the carrots, orange flower water, olive oil and orange juice.

4. Sprinkle with sea salt and freshly ground pepper, garnish with coriander and serve.

goodfood

Spinach, chilli and sesame salad

Easy
Vegan
🕐 **less than 30 mins**
Serves 4

2 bunches English spinach leaves,
   washed and trimmed
1½ tbsp peanut oil
6 dried long red chillies
2 tsp rice wine vinegar
½ tsp light soy sauce, plus extra
   to serve
2 tsp caster sugar
½ tsp sesame oil
½ tsp chilli oil
1 tbsp roasted sesame seeds,
   to serve

Most leafy greens are great in this salad and the dressing is also perfect for cos lettuce leaves. Serve with steamed rice for a simple but delicious meal.

1. Plunge the spinach into a saucepan of boiling salted water and blanch for a minute, just to wilt the leaves. Refresh under cold running water and squeeze dry.

2. Heat a wok over high heat until smoking and add the peanut oil. Reduce the heat to medium and stir-fry the chillies for about 10 seconds, until fragrant. Remove from the wok, and set aside.

3. In a large bowl, whisk the vinegar, soy, sugar and both oils, then season to taste. Add the blanched spinach and fried chillies. Gently combine, place into a large bowl to share, scatter with sesame seeds and serve with extra soy sauce on the side for drizzling.

◆ **Note** This dish works as the perfect side to steamed, blue-eye trevalla.

Chinese-style coleslaw with Asian herbs

With its piquant dressing and masses of fresh herbs, this vibrant salad makes a refreshing side dish during hot weather. For a truly unique taste of Australia, add finger limes, native karkalla (pigface), Bower spinach or samphire.

Vegan
Easy
○ less than 30 mins
Serves 4 as a side dish

1 small cucumber
3 small carrots, peeled
1 tsp white sugar
1 tsp sea salt
2 sticks celery, finely sliced on the diagonal
½ cup malt vinegar
2 tbsp white sugar, extra
2½ cups finely shredded Chinese white cabbage
⅔ cup julienned spring onions
1¼ cup fresh bean sprouts
¼ cup round leaf mint leaves
¼ cup Vietnamese mint leaves
¼ cup sweet Thai basil leaves
¼ cup coriander leaves
2 tbsp light soy sauce
2 tbsp lemon juice
2 tsp roasted sesame seeds
pinch Sichuan pepper and salt (see recipe below)

Sichuan pepper and salt
1 tbsp Sichuan peppercorns
3 tbsp sea salt

1. Using a vegetable peeler, finely slice cucumber and carrots lengthways into ribbons. Set cucumber aside and cut carrots into a fine julienne. Combine carrots in a bowl with sugar and salt, mix well and leave to stand for 15 minutes.

2. Add celery to a small saucepan of boiling salted water and blanch for 30 seconds. Drain, refresh under cold water and drain again. Set aside.

3. Combine vinegar and extra sugar in a small, heavy-based saucepan and stir over heat until sugar dissolves. Simmer, uncovered for about a minute or until slightly reduced. Set aside to cool before stirring through pickled carrot.

4. **To make the Sichuan pepper and salt,** dry-roast peppercorns and salt in a heavy-based pan. When the peppercorns begin to pop and become aromatic, take off the heat. Allow to cool, then grind to a powder in a mortar and pestle or a spice grinder (makes 4 tablespoons).

5. In a bowl, combine reserved cucumber, pickled carrot mixture, celery, cabbage, spring onion, bean sprouts and herbs. Pour over combined soy sauce and lemon juice and mix well. Arrange in a salad bowl, sprinkle with roasted sesame seeds, Sichuan pepper and salt and serve immediately.

◆ **Tip** Add some sliced, poached lobster (shown in image, right), prawns or poached chicken to this refreshing coleslaw.

Stir-fried iceberg lettuce

Easy
Vegan
🕐 **less than 30 mins**
Serves 4

2 tbsp vegetable oil
5 cloves garlic, smashed
1 small iceberg lettuce, cut into
    quarters, washed and dried
1 tbsp shaoxing
1 tbsp light soy sauce
¾ tsp sugar
pinch of sea salt
1 tsp sesame oil

I love stir-fried lettuce – it's great just with oyster sauce or XO but can also make up a delicious meal alongside your Asian-style main and steamed rice.

1. Heat a wok until just smoking. Add the oil and, when hot, add the garlic and stir-fry for 10–20 seconds or until fragrant. Add the lettuce and stir-fry for 1–2 minutes or until it becomes limp.

2. Deglaze the wok with the shaoxing, then add the soy sauce, sugar and salt and cook until the lettuce is tender. Remove from the heat and toss with sesame oil to serve.

Mexican cannellini bean salad with lime and haloumi

This salad is big on flavour and can either be served as a side with tacos or used as a filling.

Easy
Vegetarian
🕐 **less than 30 mins**
Serves 6–8

¼ cup lime juice
¼ cup olive oil
1 clove garlic, minced
1 tsp Tabasco
2 x 400g cans cannellini beans,
   rinsed and drained
1 red capsicum, cut into ½ cm dice
1 yellow capsicum, cut into
   ½ cm dice
1 red onion, finely diced
1 avocado, cut into 1cm dice
½ cup finely shredded coriander
   leaves
salt and black pepper, to season
100g haloumi

1. Whisk the lime juice, olive oil, garlic and Tabasco in a large bowl.

2. Add the remaining ingredients except for the haloumi. Mix until well combined and season with salt and pepper to taste.

3. Using a microplane, finely grate the haloumi into fluffy shreds to cover the top of the salad. Serve.

ANDREW
McCONNELL

Red endive, beetroot, juniper and horseradish cream

Vegetarian
🕐 **30 mins–1 hour**
Serves 4

2 medium or 1 large beetroot
2 heads of red endive

Beetroot juice dressing
¼ cup beetroot juice
1 tbsp red wine vinegar
4 juniper berries, crushed
1 tsp brown sugar
2 tbsp grapeseed oil
1 tsp walnut oil
salt, to taste

Horseradish cream
1 tbsp mayonnaise
1 tbsp creme fraiche
½ tbsp freshly grated horseradish
(or substitute ½ tbsp prepared
horseradish from a jar)
pinch salt and white pepper,
to taste

Beetroot has become an indispensable vegetable in my kitchen, raw or cooked. I like to use medium to small beetroot – large older beetroots can become a bit too earthy and bitter in flavour for my liking. To make the dressing for this salad you will need a quarter of a cup of beetroot juice. This is best extracted using a juice extractor. If you don't have one, your local juice shop should be able to sell you a small cup of fresh beetroot juice.

1. Place whole beetroots in a small saucepan of cold water over high heat and bring to a simmer. Reduce heat to low and cook for 15–25 minutes or until tender when pierced with a skewer.

2. **To make the beetroot juice dressing,** take a small stainless steel saucepan, add the beetroot juice, vinegar, juniper berries and sugar and bring to a simmer. Continue to simmer for a few minutes or until the beetroot juice is reduced to 2 tablespoons of liquid. Strain the beetroot juice and transfer to a small bowl. Add the grapeseed oil and walnut oil, season with a little salt and set aside at room temperature until ready to serve.

3. **To make the horseradish cream,** whisk together the mayonnaise, creme fraiche and horseradish, season with a little salt and pepper. Reserve the horseradish cream in the fridge until ready to serve. Cut the base of the endive from the bunch and remove all the individual leaves. Wash the leaves in cold water, dry in a salad spinner, then pat dry with a clean tea towel and place in a small bowl.

4. When the beetroot is cooked, remove from the water and set aside until cool enough to handle. Peel and slice the beetroot into 1cm discs or wedges. Arrange the beetroot pieces on a plate and season with a little salt and black pepper.

5. Spoon the horseradish cream over the beetroot. Dress the endive leaves with 1 tablespoon of the beetroot juice dressing. Stack the endive pieces on the beetroot and drizzle the remaining beetroot dressing over the leaves. Serve immediately.

◆ **Tip** Many heirloom beetroot varieties such as golden or chioggia (candy stripe) bring colour and in some cases a subtle and almost sweet flavour.

Ratatouille salad with olives and basil

Vegan
🕐 **1–2 hours**
Serves 4

Look for vegetables with roughly the same diameter and this will look spectacular. Serve hot with pork sausages, grilled lamb or scrambled eggs, or cool and serve as a roast vegetable salad, topped with basil, olives and capers.

1 red onion, halved and finely sliced
3 tbsp extra virgin olive oil
6 medium tomatoes
3 Lebanese (long) eggplant
3 zucchini
2 cloves garlic, finely sliced
pinch dried chilli flakes
1 tbsp thyme leaves
1 tbsp rosemary sprigs
6 cherry tomatoes, halved
2 tbsp black olives
1 tbsp capers, rinsed
handful of basil leaves

1. Preheat oven to 200°C. Toss the onion with 1 tablespoon of the oil and place in an oiled 23cm ceramic or earthenware pie dish. Slice tomatoes, eggplant and zucchini into 1cm-thick slices. Season well.

2. Using the larger slices first, arrange vegetables vertically in a ring around the edge of the dish, alternating eggplant, tomato and zucchini. Use the smaller slices to make a second concentric ring in the centre, filling the dish completely. Smoosh the vegetables with the palm of your hand so they lie at an angle like dominoes.

3. Scatter with sliced garlic, chilli flakes, thyme and rosemary and drizzle with remaining oil. Cover tightly with aluminium foil and bake for 1 hour, then remove foil and bake for a further 30 minutes or until vegetables are soft. Cool to room temperature and scatter with cherry tomatoes, olives, capers and basil to serve.

Stir-fried eggplant with chilli and ginger

Vegan
🕐 **30 mins–1 hour**
Serves 4–6

400g Japanese eggplants
3 tbsp peanut oil
5cm piece ginger, finely sliced
3 cloves garlic, roughly crushed
¼ cup shaoxing wine
1 tbsp brown sugar
2 tbsp malt vinegar
1 tbsp light soy sauce
1 tsp sesame oil
1 large red chilli, finely sliced
   lengthways

We Chinese cooks love to prepare eggplant in many different ways: braised, pickled, steamed, grilled, smoked, roasted or simply stir-fried, as in this recipe. Roughly sliced regular eggplants are fine to use instead of Japanese eggplants.

1. Remove stems from eggplants and cut diagonally into 1cm slices.

2. Heat 2 tablespoons of the peanut oil in a hot wok until the surface seems to shimmer slightly. Add eggplant and stir-fry for about 2½ minutes, being careful not to let it burn.

3. Add remaining peanut oil to wok with ginger and garlic and stir-fry for a further minute.

4. Add shaoxing wine and sugar and stir-fry for one minute. Add remaining ingredients and stir-fry for a further minute. Serve immediately.

◆ **Note** This rich and intensely flavoured dish makes a great accompaniment to a more delicately flavoured dish such as steamed snapper with ginger and shallots, or alongside fried rice for a simple and quick meal. You can substitute a splash of leftover red or white wine for the shaoxing – a hint of alcohol adds depth and character.

KATRINA MEYNINK

Sweet potato chaat with coconut, mint and lime sambal

Vegan
🕐 **45 mins**
Serves 4

A good ol' tray of roasted veg isn't just for autumn and winter. Loaded and adorned with herbs, spices and nuts, roasted vegies are something to be enjoyed just as much when the weather warms. This dish works both as a side or as the star of your meal. If you can't find tamarind chutney, use about 2 teaspoons of tamarind extract and double the amount of brown sugar to achieve a balance of tart and sweet.

Sweet potato
800g sweet potato, peeled and
    quartered lengthways
1½ tbsp rice bran oil
2 tsp brown sugar
5 tbsp tamarind chutney
salt and pepper, to season
juice of ½ lime
1 tsp chaat masala

Coconut, mint and lime sambal
40g fresh coconut, grated or thinly
    sliced on a mandolin
1 cup mint leaves
½ cup coriander leaves
1 long green chilli, sliced
juice and zest of 1 lime

Topping
½ cup puffed buckwheat
1 tsp chaat masala
seeds of ½ pomegranate
½ red onion, finely sliced
brown sugar, to taste

1. Preheat oven to 180°C and line a large baking tray with baking paper.

2. Combine sweet potato ingredients in a large bowl and toss to coat. Turn out onto prepared tray and roast for 35-45 minutes or until tender and brown.

3. Meanwhile, place the sambal ingredients in a blender, pulse briefly, and season to taste – don't blitz it so much that it turns into a paste, but the herbs and coconut should meld together. Set aside until ready to serve.

4. Combine the topping ingredients in a bowl. Taste and add a sprinkle of brown sugar if it is too tart (chaat masala spice mix can vary – some combinations include asafoetida which can add to the tang/sourness).

5. Place the sweet potato on a serving plate, top with dollops of coconut sambal, scatter the puffed buckwheat topping and serve.

KATRINA MEYNINK

Beetroot, feta and orange salad with cayenne and rosewater dressing

Add a fragrant floral touch and a touch of spice to a classic beetroot and feta salad with this vibrant recipe.

Easy
Gluten-free
🕐 **less than 30 mins**
Serves 4–6

Salad

4 beetroot, peeled and shredded (use a grater if you don't have a food processor)

2 oranges, peeled and chopped into bite-sized pieces

1 cup mint leaves, coarsely torn

½ cup Persian-style (soft) feta

Dressing

½ tsp cayenne pepper (or to taste)

3 tbsp rosewater

2 tbsp pomegranate molasses

½ cup grapeseed oil

1 tbsp dried edible rose petals

1 tbsp rapadura (panela) sugar

juice and zest of 1 lemon

1. Add all the salad ingredients to a serving bowl and using your hands, gently toss to combine – you don't want the beetroot colour to bleed all over the orange and feta.

2. Combine the dressing ingredients and drizzle over the salad, just enough to coat. Toss gently, season with salt and pepper and serve immediately.

good food

Farro salad

Easy
Vegan
🕐 **less than 30 mins**
Serves 4

175g farro*
3 handfuls flat-leaf parsley,
  finely shredded
1 handful mint, finely shredded
1 small red onion, finely diced
3 spring onions, sliced into
  fine rounds
3 vine-ripened tomatoes, peeled,
  de-seeded and finely diced
125ml extra virgin olive oil
Juice of 2 lemons
sea salt and freshly ground pepper

*Farro is available from selected
  delicatessens. Pearl farro will
  take less time to cook than
  whole and roasted farro.

You can use any grain, or a mix of grains (perhaps quinoa, bulgur wheat or brown rice), for this salad that bursts with colour, flavour and freshness.

1. Bring a large saucepan of salted water to the boil, pour in the farro and cook for 10-20 minutes or until just tender. Drain and spread out on a tray to cool.

2. Put the farro in a bowl and add all the remaining ingredients except for the extra virgin olive oil, lemon juice and seasoning. Mix well, then add the dressing and mix thoroughly. Check the seasoning and adjust to taste.

3. Place on a large platter to serve as part of a mezze table, or spoon onto a plate and serve with roasted or barbecued meat or seafood.

Vegies, sides and salads

ANDREW
McCONNELL

Easy
Vegetarian
⏱ **less than 30 mins**
Serves 4

4 tbsp butter
4 cloves garlic, grated on
   a microplane
handful parsley leaves, chopped
salt and pepper, to season
zest of ½ lemon
4 large field mushrooms
8 sprigs thyme

Foil-baked field mushrooms with garlic, butter and thyme

These garlicky mushrooms are perfect served alone or as an accompaniment to a main course. I recently cooked these for dinner at home. I made an extra cheesy risotto with plenty of parmesan and mascarpone cheese and placed a baked mushroom on top of each serving and spooned all the baking juices over. It's comforting, delicious and vegetarian.

1. Preheat oven to 180°C. Place butter and garlic in a medium bowl. Add parsley, lemon zest and a pinch of salt and pepper. Stir the butter well to incorporate the ingredients.

2. Peel mushrooms and trim the stalk with a paring knife. Smear the garlic butter evenly over all the mushroom gills, place 2 sprigs of thyme on each and season.

3. Place each of the mushrooms in the centre of a 30cm square of aluminium foil. Fold corners up and seal edges. Place on a baking tray and cook for 15-20 minutes.

4. Carefully open parcels, transfer mushrooms to serving plates and spoon over any of the cooking juices to serve.

Eggplant and chickpea fetteh

Easy
Vegetarian
🕐 **30 mins–1 hour**
Serves 4

2 tbsp vegetable oil
1 small eggplant, cut into
    5cm cubes
1 red onion, peeled, chopped
2 cloves garlic, peeled, sliced
2 large pita bread

Topping
1 tsp paprika
1 tsp ground cumin
¼ cup pistachio kernels,
    roughly chopped
¼ cup almonds, roughly chopped

Yoghurt
1½ cups plain yoghurt
2 cloves garlic, crushed
400g can chickpeas, rinsed
    thoroughly
salt and pepper, to season
juice and zest of ½ lemon
4 tbsp chopped fresh mint
1 heaped tbsp tahini

Use the right yoghurt – one with plenty of creaminess and tang – and this fetteh is perfect comfort fodder for your belly.

1. Preheat oven to 175°C. Add oil, eggplant, onion and garlic to a roasting dish and toss to coat. Roast, shaking the dish occasionally to prevent the garlic catching, for about 30 minutes or until golden.

2. Toss the topping ingredients together in a small bowl. Set aside.

3. Combine yoghurt and garlic in a bowl then add to a saucepan with the chickpeas. Season with salt and pepper. Place over low heat and cook until chickpeas are warmed through (about a minute). Be careful to keep the heat on low so that the yoghurt mixture doesn't separate. Add the eggplant mixture and stir until just coated, then stir through the lemon juice and zest, mint and tahini.

4. Add your pita bread to the oven for 1-2 minutes or until just crisp. Break the bread into pieces and divide between 4 bowls. Spoon chickpea-eggplant mixture into the bowls and finish with a generous spoonful (about 2 tablespoons per serve) of the topping and serve.

goodfood

Stir-fried chickpeas with black bean and chilli

Easy
Vegan
🕐 **1–2 hours**
Serves 4

1 cup (200g) dried chickpeas
3 tbsp peanut oil
2cm piece ginger, julienned
2 cloves garlic, roughly diced
2 tbsp salted black beans
1 small red onion, finely sliced
½ medium red capsicum, seeds
   and membrane removed,
   julienned
3 tbsp shaoxing wine
2 tsp brown sugar
2 tbsp tamari
1 tbsp brown rice vinegar
½ tsp sesame oil
2 spring onions, finely sliced
1 long red chilli, finely sliced

With the hearty texture and nutty, creamy flavour of chickpeas soaking up piquant, complex flavours and aromas of fermented black beans and chilli, this is an excellent vegetarian option served on its own with steamed jasmine rice, or as a side dish with poached chicken.

1. Soak chickpeas overnight in plenty of cold water.

2. The following day, drain chickpeas, place in a saucepan and cover with cold water. Bring to the boil, then simmer over a low-moderate heat for about 45 minutes or until tender. Allow to cool in their cooking water, then drain. Set aside.

3. Heat peanut oil in a wok until surface seems to shimmer slightly. Add ginger, garlic, black beans, onion and capsicum and cook for 2 minutes or until fragrant. Add chickpeas and stir-fry for 2 minutes.

4. Add wine, drizzling it around the sides of the wok in a circular motion, then add sugar, tamari, vinegar and sesame oil and cook for 3 minutes to create a rich sauce. Toss in spring onion and chilli and serve immediately.

Garam masala roasted cauliflower steaks in coconut and saffron curry

Easy
Vegan
🕐 **30 mins – 1 hour**
Serves 4

½ large head of cauliflower, cut into
  3cm-thick steaks
1 tbsp rice bran oil
1 tbsp garam masala
6-8 kale leaves
½ tsp saffron threads
¼ cup canola oil
1 tbsp cumin seeds
400g can pureed tomatoes
1 tbsp brown mustard seeds,
  ground
½ tsp fenugreek seeds, ground
1 tsp cayenne pepper
1 tsp turmeric
1 tsp salt
2 cups vegetable stock
400ml can coconut milk
seeds of ½ pomegranate
fresh mint leaves
1 green chilli, finely sliced

Try to find a bold garam masala – one with the smoky goodness of cumin and coriander seeds – or make your own. The spice mix is the perfect partner for cauliflower and holds its own before being pelted with hits of glorious saffron and creamy coconut.

1. Preheat oven to 180°C and line a roasting tray with baking paper.

2. Gently rub cauliflower steaks with the rice bran oil and garam masala and arrange on prepared tray. Roast for 30 minutes or until the cauliflower is golden and cooked through. For the last 2 minutes of cooking time, add the kale leaves and roast until crisp. Set aside. Soak saffron in ¼ cup of warm water and set aside.

3. While the cauliflower is roasting, heat canola oil over high heat in a medium saucepan for 1 minute. Add cumin seeds and cook for about 30 seconds. Reduce heat to medium, add tomatoes, mustard seeds, fenugreek, cayenne, turmeric and salt. Stir well and cook for 5 minutes or until oil glistens on the tomatoes.

4. Add stock and bring to the boil. Reduce heat to medium-low and cook for 10 minutes, stirring regularly. Add coconut milk, reserving about 2 tablespoons for serving, and saffron (including its water). Stir well and cook for a further 15 minutes.

5. Place cauliflower steaks in bowls and top with curry sauce. Pour over the remaining 2 tablespoons of coconut milk and scatter with crisp kale leaves, pomegranate, mint and chilli to serve.

Salt and vinegar crispy potatoes

Easy
Vegan
🕐 **1–2 hours**
Serves 6–8

1kg potatoes, peeled and cut
  into chunks
1 tsp salt
1 cup white vinegar, plus extra
  to serve
1 cup vegetable oil
sea salt, to season

This is a perfect chip flavour for me, and there isn't much you need to do to improve it. You could use fancy vinegars and add other flavours if you like but really, what's the point? If it ain't broke, don't fix it.

1. Preheat oven to 220°C. Place potato in a large saucepan and add the salt and vinegar, then cover with cold water. Place the saucepan over medium heat and bring to the boil, then reduce heat to a simmer and cook for about 15 minute or until a small sharp knife can be inserted and withdrawn easily. Drain well and return the potato to the warm, empty saucepan. Heat over very low heat for a few more minutes to expel excess moisture from the potato.

2. Meanwhile, place the vegetable oil in a large roasting tray and heat in the oven. Add potato to the oil and stir to coat. Roast for 45 minutes–1 hour, stirring occasionally, until potato is golden brown and crisp. Season well with salt and sprinkle with a little extra vinegar if you like.

DANIELLE ALVAREZ

Brown butter and citrus roasted carrots

This is a beautiful accompaniment to roast chicken or you could swap the labna for some browned haloumi to make a more substantial vegetarian dish.

Easy
Vegetarian
🕐 **30 mins–1 hour**
Serves 4–6

2 bunches Dutch carrots
1 tbsp extra virgin olive oil
salt, to season
80g butter
zest of ½ lemon
zest of ½ lime
zest of ½ orange
6 sprigs thyme, leaves picked and
    stalks discarded
1 tbsp honey
juice from ½ lemon
200g labna

1. Preheat oven to 200°C. Wash and scrub the carrots and cut off the green tops, if they have them. Drizzle with olive oil and sprinkle with salt. Roast for 30-45 minutes, depending on their size, until completely soft and caramelised all over.

2. Meanwhile, put the butter in a pan over medium heat and allow it to melt and turn into brown butter, swirling the pan occasionally so it cooks evenly. When the butter has coloured to nut brown, remove it from the heat and add the citrus zest and thyme (be careful as it will splatter). Add the honey and lemon juice. Mix to combine and keep warm until ready to serve.

3. Spread the labna on a serving platter and top with the carrots and brown butter sauce. Finish with a sprinkle of sea salt to serve.

Green noodle bowl with broccoli

Easy
Vegan
🕐 **less than 30 mins**
Serves 4

800g broccoli (two heads)
1 bunch kale
200g edamame
200g silken tofu, rinsed and diced
200g cha soba (green tea noodles)
Japanese togarashi sprinkles,
    to taste

Sesame seed dressing
2 tbsp rice vinegar
4 tbsp tamari or soy
1 tbsp maple syrup
1 tsp sesame oil
2 tbsp sesame seeds, toasted

Turn broccoli into a star three times over – as florets, stalks and broccoli rice. Team with green tea noodles, as here, or with soba or zucchini noodles.

1. Cut florets off the broccoli, trim the stalk and finely slice crosswise into discs. Blend a handful of the florets in a small food processor until you have broccoli "rice" and set aside. Strip leaves from the kale, discarding stalks, and roughly chop.

2. To make the sesame seed dressing, whisk ingredients together in a small bowl and set aside.

3. Cook edamame in a large saucepan of salted, simmering water for 4 minutes. Scoop out, pod and set aside. Add remaining broccoli florets, sliced broccoli stalk and kale leaves to the water and cook for 3-4 minutes until just tender. Scoop out of water and drain well.

4. Add tofu to the water and simmer for 30 seconds then scoop out and drain. Place broccoli rice in a small strainer and dip into the simmering water for 30 seconds to heat through, then drain. Add noodles to the water and cook, stirring occasionally for three minutes or until tender, then drain.

5. Divide noodles between serving bowls and top with broccoli florets, stalks and "rice", kale leaves and tofu. Scatter with edamame and togarashi and serve with sesame seed dressing.

Vegies, sides and salads

goodfood

Chickpea and roast pumpkin casserole

Easy
Vegetarian
🕐 **30 mins–1 hour**
Serves 4

250g dried chickpeas, soaked
   overnight, drained
½ small pumpkin, cut into
   half-moon wedges
1 tbsp olive oil
salt and freshly ground pepper,
   to season
2 tbsp vegetable oil
1 onion, finely sliced
1 carrot, sliced
2 tbsp grated ginger
2 cloves garlic, grated
400g can cherry tomatoes
2 tbsp honey
2 cinnamon sticks
1 tsp salt
½ tsp ground pepper
1 tsp ground turmeric
1 tsp ground cumin
1 tsp ground cinnamon
1 tsp ground ginger
600ml water or stock
yoghurt, coriander and dukkah,
   to serve

Cook your chickpeas in a spicy, immune-boosting stew of garlic, ginger, turmeric, onions and carrots as pumpkins roast sweetly on another shelf, then combine at the table with yoghurt, dukkah and coriander.

1. Preheat oven to 160°C. Toss pumpkin in olive oil, season well and bake on the top shelf of the oven for 1 hour until golden.

2. Heat vegetable oil in a deep, heavy-based, lidded pan or heatproof, heavy-based casserole over medium heat. Add onion, carrot, ginger and garlic and cook for 10 minutes or until softened. Add chickpeas, tomatoes, honey, cinnamon, salt, pepper, ground spices and water and bring to the boil.

3. Cover and bake in the oven for 45 minutes, adding more water or stock as needed to keep it thick and soupy.

4. To serve, arrange roast pumpkin on top, drizzle with yoghurt, and scatter with coriander leaves and dukkah.

Sweet potato and kale bowl with quinoa, coriander-tahini dressing and crispy chilli-lime chickpeas

Healthy doesn't have to be boring. Add tahini and crispy chickpeas to your grain bowl for extra flair.

Gluten-free
🕐 **1–2 hours**
Serves 4

1 medium sweet potato (about 350g), peeled and sliced into 2cm-thick rounds
1 tbsp olive oil
1 cup tri-coloured quinoa
2 cups chicken or vegetable stock
½ head small leaf kale, rinsed, leaves separated
1½ avocados, sliced
2 purple carrots, peeled into strips using a mandolin or peeler
juice of 1 lime

Coriander tahini dressing (makes approx. 1 cup)
⅓ cup tahini
⅓ cup smoked almonds
4 tbsp olive oil
3 tbsp lemon juice
2 tbsp parmesan
¾ cup loosely packed coriander leaves
2 tsp soy sauce
1 clove garlic, chopped
¾ tsp chilli powder or to taste
½ tsp paprika

For the roasted chilli-lime chickpeas
400g can chickpeas, rinsed and drained thoroughly
2 tbsp olive oil
zest of 1 lime
1 tbsp lime juice
1 tbsp chilli powder
1 tsp garlic salt
½ tsp pepper

To serve
2 tbsp salad seed mix
lemon wedges and micro herbs such as dill, parsley and coriander

1. Preheat oven to 180°C and line a baking tray with baking paper. To make the chilli-lime chickpeas, toss chickpeas with oil, lime zest and juice, chilli, garlic salt and pepper and spread on prepared tray. Bake for 30 minutes, tossing halfway through cooking. Remove and set aside to cool completely (leftover roasted chickpeas will last for one week in a tightly sealed container).

2. Spread sweet potato on the same baking tray. Season generously and drizzle with olive oil. Roast for 30 minutes or until cooked through and starting to caramelise.

3. Meanwhile, gently simmer the quinoa in stock for 12 minutes. Remove from heat, cover and set aside for 10 minutes to steam and fluff up.

4. For the coriander-tahini dressing, add all ingredients to a blender and blitz to combine. If the dressing is too thick, add a tablespoon of water and blitz again. Continue until desired consistency is achieved.

5. Place kale on a baking tray lined with baking paper and roast for 5–7 minutes or until just crisp. Season generously.

6. Divide quinoa between serving bowls. Top with sweet potato, chickpeas, avocado, carrot, crispy kale and lime juice. Top with salad seeds, micro herbs and dressing. Serve with lemon wedges.

◆ **Note** Keep dressing separate if not eating immediately, and dress salad just before serving. Leftover dressing will keep for 1 week in the fridge.

Pasta, grains, eggs and tarts

ANDREW
McCONNELL

Comte cheese quiche

⏱ 2 hours
Serves 8

This recipe for me is the ultimate quiche – not an everyday quiche but one worthy of celebration. Comte is a French cooked curd cheese that is also known as comte gruyere. Good comte is aged from eight to 18 months and has a semi-firm texture and a deep nutty flavour. It is an incredible cheese to eat as is, and responds well when used in cooking. It is also one of my favourite cheeses to pair with wine.

180g cold unsalted butter, diced
240g plain flour, plus extra
   for dusting
pinch of salt
65ml water

Tart filling
2 egg yolks
4 eggs
300ml thickened cream
200g creme fraiche
175g comte gruyere, finely grated
175g parmesan, finely grated
pinch of salt and cayenne pepper

1. In a food processor, pulse butter, flour and salt a few times to form a coarse crumb. With the motor running, quickly add the water and turn off the machine. Turn out dough onto a clean bench and knead gently to bring together. Don't overwork. Wrap in plastic wrap and refrigerate for at least an hour. (This step can be done a day ahead.)

2. Brush a 2.5cm-deep, 24cm round tart tin with a little melted butter. Turn out dough on a lightly floured surface and roll into a 3mm-thick round, slightly larger than the prepared tin. Carefully lay dough round in the tart tin, pressing into the corners and leaving any excess dough hanging over the edges. Pierce the base a few times with a fork and refrigerate for an hour.

3. Preheat oven to 170°C. Line tart case with baking paper and fill with rice or rock salt. Bake for 30 minutes, carefully remove the rice or rock salt and baking paper and return to the oven for a further 10-15 minutes or until golden. If the pastry still feels a little moist, cook for a further 5 minutes. Remove from the oven and trim overhanging edges with a serrated knife.

4. Reduce oven temperature to 140°C. Whisk egg yolks, eggs, cream and creme fraiche in a large mixing bowl. Fold in the cheeses and season with salt and pepper. Place the cooked tart shell in the oven on a baking tray (this will help avoid spills). Pour the egg mixture into the shell and bake for 20 minutes, then reduce temperature to 120°C and cook for a further 30 minutes or until cooked (tap the tray gently to check if filling has set – it should wobble as one). Serve.

goodfood

DANIELLE ALVAREZ

Beetroot tarte tatin with rye crust

Vegetarian
🕐 **2 hours**
Serves 8–10

Although tarte tatin is typically a dessert, this version is decidedly savoury. Sure, there is sweetness in the honey and beetroot but I counter that with acidity from the vinegar, nuttiness from the rye and creamy sourness from the goat's curd. I would serve this as a wintry vegetarian lunch with a hearty rocket or radicchio salad.

26–35 baby red beetroot (about
   6 bunches), washed and trimmed
3 tbsp olive oil
salt, to season
100g honey
4 tbsp chardonnay vinegar
100g goat's curd, to serve

Dough
200g plain flour
140g rye flour
1½ tsp salt
1 tbsp sugar
225g cold diced butter
130-140ml cold water

1. To make the dough, place the flours, salt and sugar in a bowl and mix to combine. Using your fingertips, rub the butter into the flour until you are left with shaggy pieces of butter mixed with flour. The biggest chunks of butter should be no larger than a pea. Add water a little at a time. When you have added nearly all the water, give the dough a good knead. If it holds together well and there is no flour left in the bottom of the bowl, stop there. If the dough still looks crumbly, add a bit more water and knead again. The goal is to have a dough that holds together without looking cracked or dry while not being over-kneaded. If you still see bits of butter in the finished dough, that's a good sign. Form the dough into a disc, wrap in plastic wrap and refrigerate for at least an hour or overnight. Or, you can freeze the dough for later.

2. Preheat oven to 200°C and place a baking stone in the oven, if you have one. Place beetroot in a shallow baking tray. Add oil, a splash of water and some salt and shake to coat the beetroot. Cover with aluminium foil and bake for 40–50 minutes or until tender when pierced with a small knife. Allow to cool then rub to remove skins (or peel if they don't come off easily). Trim beetroot so they are flat and roughly the same height.

3. Heat honey and vinegar in a 20cm ovenproof cast-iron pan until bubbly, then place all the beetroot into the pan, flat-side down. Squeeze in as many as possible – the tart is more impressive if the beetroot are packed in tightly. Sprinkle them with a bit of salt.

4. Remove dough from fridge and roll out as thinly as possible. Place over the beetroot with the edges hanging over the pan. Using scissors, cut around the edge of the pan, leaving a 2cm overhang. Save excess dough for another use or discard. Tuck the overhanging pastry around the beetroot into the pan. Cut a small slit in the centre of the dough to allow steam to escape.

5. Bake for 35–45 minutes or until golden. Allow to cool for 2–3 minutes, loosen the edges with a knife, and carefully flip on to a serving platter. Serve warm or at room temperature, dotting the top with goat's curd.

◆ **Tip** Save the beet greens, too. They make an excellent addition to a frittata or sauteed as a side dish alongside the protein of your choice.

Carrot and caraway tarte tatin with herbed yoghurt and horseradish

Vegetarian
🕐 **1–2 hours**
Serves 4–6

1 tsp caraway seeds
1 tsp coriander seeds
extra virgin olive oil
2 red onions, peeled and
    thinly sliced
1 tbsp brown sugar
2 tbsp apple cider vinegar
200g mixed heirloom carrots
⅓ cup soft Persian-style feta
large sheet pre-rolled puff pastry,
    cut to fit roasting dish

Herbed yoghurt
¼ cup Greek-style yoghurt
1 tsp each chopped flat-leaf
    parsley, mint, dill, tarragon,
    chives
zest and juice of 1 lime
1 tbsp extra virgin olive oil
salt and pepper, to season

To serve
40g fresh horseradish*, grated on
    a microplane
chervil sprigs

*If you can't find fresh horseradish,
mix 1 tsp prepared horseradish
(you'll find it in the supermarket
condiment section) into the
herbed yoghurt mixture.

You'll need a high-sided roasting dish about 36cm x 13cm to make this tart.

1. **To make the herbed yoghurt,** combine the yoghurt, herbs, lime zest and juice and olive oil in a medium bowl. Season generously with salt and pepper and set aside.

2. Place a small frying pan over medium heat. Add the caraway and coriander and cook, stirring often to prevent catching, for about 1 minute or until fragrant. Transfer to a mortar and pestle and roughly grind – you still want some texture.

3. Wipe out the frying pan with paper towel and return to the heat, turning heat to medium-low. Drizzle in some olive oil then add the onion and gently cook until soft and translucent. Add the brown sugar and apple cider vinegar and continue to cook until a jam-like consistency is achieved. Set aside.

4. **For the roasted carrots,** preheat oven to 180°C. Add the carrots to a high-sided roasting tray and drizzle with olive oil. Scatter over the toasted spices, season with salt and pepper and toss carrots to coat. Pour about 100ml water into the tray, cover with foil and roast for 20 minutes.

5. Remove foil and roast for a further 15 minutes, until the carrots are tender and the water has evaporated.

6. Remove the tray from the oven and dollop the onion relish over the carrots. Don't worry about being uniform – the pockets of surprise are what make this tart. Similarly, dollop over the feta in random spots before encasing the carrots in the pastry, tucking it around the edges as you would a bed.

7. Cook in the oven for 40 minutes or until the pastry is puffed and golden. Try to be patient, if you remove it too early the pastry will be soggy in the middle.

8. Loosen around the edges with a knife and carefully flip the tart onto a serving platter. Drizzle over the herbed yoghurt then sprinkle over the fresh horseradish and chervil. Serve immediately.

goodfood

KATRINA MEYNINK

Pasta with tomato vodka sauce, chilli and burrata

Easy
Vegetarian
🕐 **30 mins**
Serves 4

4 fresh red chillies
2 tsp olive oil
1 onion, finely chopped
2 cloves garlic, crushed
200ml tomato passata
salt and pepper, to season
10–12 basil leaves
about 100g–150g pasta per serve
    (use a thick flat-style pasta that
    will catch the sauce and melted
    cheese)
1 cup good-quality semi-dried
    smoked tomatoes, roughly
    chopped
½ cup bocconcini balls
¼ cup vodka
1 ball burrata or buffalo mozzarella
    and micro herbs, to serve

There have been many claims to the invention of the more traditional parent to this number, penne alla vodka, but whatever its origins, the subtle kick of vodka lifts the most simple of tomato sauce and pasta combinations. Skip the roasted chillies for five-minute midweek saviour cooking at its finest.

1. Preheat oven to 190°C–200°C. Place the chillies on a lightly oiled baking tray and roast for 10–15 minutes, or until skins are thoroughly blackened. Flip to expose the other side and cook for a further 5–10 minutes or until skins are thoroughly charred. Remove and set aside.

2. **To make the tomato sauce**, heat the olive oil in a small saucepan. Add the onion and garlic and fry gently until golden. Add the passata and season with salt and pepper. Add several fresh basil leaves and cook gently for about 10 minutes.

3. While the sauce is simmering, bring a large saucepan of water to the boil, add salt and cook the pasta until al dente. Drain well.

4. Add the semi-dried tomatoes, bocconcini and vodka to the sauce. Return to low heat until the cheese just starts to string and melt. Add the drained pasta and shake the pan to coat the pasta in sauce.

5. Remove from heat, divide among 4 serving bowls and top each with a coarsely torn piece of burrata or mozzarella, a roasted chilli and micro herbs. Serve piping hot.

DANIELLE ALVAREZ

Rigatoni with smoky eggplant, tomato and oregano

Vegetarian
🕐 **1–2 hours**
Serves 4–6

2 medium-sized purple eggplants
100ml extra virgin olive oil, plus
    extra as needed
4 cloves garlic, smashed
½ tsp dried chilli flakes
2 punnets (about 400g) cherry
    tomatoes
6 stems fresh oregano, leaves
    picked, plus extra to serve
450g rigatoni
½ lemon
about 50g ricotta salata, crumbled
about 60g freshly grated parmesan

In Italy, this combination of eggplant, tomato and ricotta salata is known as "pasta alla Norma", supposedly named after the opera by Sicilian composer Bellini. I like the idea of naming a combination of humble ingredients after one of the most celebrated operas of the early 19th century. How grand! Here, I'm charring the eggplant to add an appealing element of smokiness. Combined with a salad and a dessert, this vegetarian pasta is a standout main course for entertaining.

1. Take 1 of the eggplants, prick it a few times with a fork or skewer and char it over a gas flame or grill. It should be completely blackened outside and soft on the inside. If the skin gets completely black but it's not yet soft in the middle, finish roasting it in a 180°C oven until softened. Set aside and allow to cool.

2. Meanwhile, cut remaining eggplant into medium-sized chunks. Heat oil in a wide, deep heavy-bottomed pan until hot, then add eggplant. Make sure the heat is on high when the eggplant goes in and then immediately turn it down to medium-high. Season the eggplant and brown it on a few sides. Some will stick and that's OK. As with browning meat, the trick is not to shake it around straight away. Drop it in, make sure it's in an even layer, then leave it for a few minutes. The eggplant will absorb a lot of the oil so you may need to add a bit more (which you can always remove later). It will brown, then start to release from the pan. Once it softens it will stick a bit more. That's OK, too. Once most of the eggplant is soft and brown, remove from the pan onto a plate lined with paper towel.

3. In the same pan, add a bit more oil if pan is dry and sizzle the garlic until fragrant. Add chilli, tomatoes and oregano and season again. Turn heat to medium and allow the tomatoes to cook gently without burning the garlic – they will soon begin to burst and release their juice. Set aside.

4. Meanwhile, take the smoky eggplant and peel away all the charred skin and stem. Chop the fleshy interior as finely as possible or throw in the food processor to make your life easier. Set aside.

5. Cook pasta in boiling salted water to your liking. Scoop the pasta out of the pot and into the pan with tomatoes. Place over medium heat and fold in eggplant puree, browned eggplant and a ladleful of pasta water. Toss to combine (the tossing motion is not just to impress your friends: it emulsifies the starches in the pasta and water to create a beautiful coating on your pasta). Add more pasta water to loosen the sauce if necessary.

6. Check for seasoning and add a squeeze of lemon to taste. Top with a drizzle of oil, ricotta salata, parmesan and fresh oregano to serve.

Roasted broccoli, chilli and ricotta cake

Vegetarian
🕐 **1–2 hours**
Serves 6

Imagine if the ubiquitous zucchini slice and everyone's favourite Ottolenghi salad, char-grilled broccoli and chilli, had a baby. This is what you'd get. My teenage nephew, who claims to hate broccoli as well as eggs, reluctantly tasted this when I gave my sister the recipe. He had the leftovers for lunch the next day.

300g broccoli, florets and stems
   cut into 2-3cm pieces
140ml extra virgin olive oil
2½ tsp sea salt flakes
freshly ground black pepper
2 large cloves garlic, peeled, halved
   lengthwise, then thinly sliced
1½ long, mild red chillies,
   thinly sliced
1 small onion, peeled and grated
1 lemon, zested
4 eggs, lightly beaten
40g finely grated parmesan, plus
   1 tbsp extra, for sprinkling
200g ricotta cheese
120g self-raising flour
salt and freshly ground pepper,
   to season

1. Preheat oven to 220°C (200°C fan-forced). Line the base of a 20cm round springform cake tin with baking paper.

2. Bring a large saucepan of water to the boil and blanch the broccoli for 1 minute. Drain and transfer to a large oven tray and toss with 2 tablespoons of the extra virgin olive oil, 1 teaspoon of salt flakes and a few turns of the pepper mill. Place in the oven and roast for 10 minutes, then set aside to cool. Reduce the oven temperature to 200°C (180°C fan-forced).

3. While the broccoli is roasting, pour the remaining olive oil (you should have about 100ml) into a small saucepan, add the garlic and half the chilli, then place over low heat to infuse. When the garlic just begins to colour, about 10 minutes, remove from the heat and set aside to cool to room temperature. Remember that the garlic will continue to cook off the stove, so don't allow it to get too brown before removing from the heat. Once cool, strain the oil and discard the garlic and chilli.

4. In a large bowl, combine roasted broccoli, onion and lemon zest. Add the eggs, the cooled infused olive oil and the grated parmesan, then crumble over the ricotta and season with 1½ teaspoons of sea salt flakes. Add flour and fold gently until just combined.

5. Scrape the mixture into prepared tin and use a small spatula to smooth the surface. Sprinkle over the extra parmesan and the remaining chilli. Cook in the oven for 35 minutes or until a skewer inserted into the middle comes out clean. Allow to cool for 15 minutes before transferring to a serving plate.

◆ **Tip** The cake is best served warm or at room temperature. It can also be wrapped in aluminium foil and refrigerated for up to 3 days.

KATRINA MEYNINK

Turkish poached egg, baharat spiced cauliflower, loaded hummus and lentil-quinoa salad

Healthy doesn't have to be boring. Grain bowls are a treat for your health and your taste-buds.

Vegetarian
🕐 **30 mins–1 hour**
Serves 4

½ large head cauliflower, cut through the stalk into 4 thick slices
1 tbsp baharat spice mix
1 tbsp olive oil
salt and pepper, to season

Lentil and quinoa salad
1 cup tri-coloured quinoa, cooked according to packet instructions
½ cup French-style lentils, cooked according to packet instructions
1 tbsp pomegranate molasses

Loaded hummus
1 cup hummus
½ punnet (125g) strawberries, sliced
½ punnet (125g) cherry tomatoes, diced
few sprigs of dill and flat leaf parsley, finely chopped

Turkish poached egg
1 cup plain full-fat Greek yoghurt
1 tbsp finely chopped dill
2 cloves garlic, crushed
4 eggs
splash of white vinegar
3 tbsp butter
1 tsp Aleppo pepper (or chilli flakes or smoked paprika)
micro herbs, to serve (optional)

1. Preheat oven to 170°C. For the cauliflower, rub the spice mix and oil generously into the cauliflower slices then place on a baking tray lined with baking paper. Roast until golden brown (12 to 15 minutes), turn and roast until tender (a further 8 to 10 minutes).

2. **For the lentil and quinoa salad,** add the quinoa and lentils to a bowl with the pomegranate molasses and stir to combine. Season generously then set aside.

3. **For the loaded hummus,** add the strawberries, tomatoes and herbs to a bowl and toss to combine. Set aside.

4. **For the Turkish poached eggs,** prepare the yoghurt base by stirring the yoghurt, dill, garlic, salt and pepper in a bowl. Bring a medium saucepan of salted water to the boil. Reduce heat to medium and add splash of vinegar; using a slotted spoon, swirl water to create a whirlpool. Crack 1 egg at a time into a bowl and slide egg into water; poach until the white is firm but yolk is runny, about 3 minutes. Using slotted spoon, transfer eggs to paper towels to drain.

5. To assemble, place a dollop of the yoghurt mixture in the centre of each bowl. Top with an egg. Place a dollop of hummus next to the egg and top with the strawberry, tomato and herb mixture. Add a spoonful of the lentil-quinoa salad.

6. Melt butter in a frying pan over medium-high heat. Stir in Aleppo pepper and salt; drizzle over the egg, yoghurt and grains. Season generously, scatter with micro herbs (if using) and serve warm.

Bacon, cheddar and jalapeno bread pudding

🕐 **1–2 hours**
Serves 6

This is a dish with more heft and less faff than quiche which can be made a day ahead. Use a baking dish measuring about 23cm x 17cm. For a vegetarian version, substitute the bacon with mushrooms. Serve with a tomato and avocado salad.

1 x 500g white cob loaf
60g butter, softened, plus 20g extra
    for greasing
1 tbsp olive oil
12 rashers streaky smoked bacon
    (about 250g)
1 large onion, roughly chopped
125ml dry white vermouth (or other
    dry white wine)
2 large eggs
3 egg yolks (from large eggs)
300ml single cream
300ml sour cream
1 tsp salt
½ tsp freshly ground black pepper
80g pickled, sliced jalapenos
200g strong cheddar cheese,
    grated
3 tbsp chives, finely chopped

1. Preheat oven to 170°C (150°C fan-forced). Slice the cob loaf in half, then into 2cm-thick slices. Arrange slices in a single layer on one or two baking trays and place in the oven for about 10 minutes, turning halfway through so both sides are lightly toasted. When cooled, lightly butter 1 side of each slice and set aside.

2. Heat the oil in a large frying pan over medium heat, add bacon and cook until golden brown but not crisp. You may need to cook in batches to prevent the bacon from stewing. Transfer to a plate and set aside. Without washing the frying pan, toss in the onion and cook over medium heat until softened and lightly browned. Add the vermouth, increase the heat to medium-high and simmer until most of the liquid has evaporated. Set aside.

3. Whisk the eggs and yolks in a medium bowl, then whisk in the cream, sour cream, salt and pepper to combine. Set aside.

4. Grease the baking dish with the extra butter, then arrange half of the bread slices – buttered-side down and overlapping slightly – in the dish. Sprinkle half the onion over the bread, then roughly tear the bacon and scatter half the rashers on top. Dot with half the jalapeno, then scatter over half of the cheese and half of the chives. Repeat the layering with the remaining bread slices, onion, bacon and jalapeno (the remaining cheese and chives will be used later). Ladle the egg mixture evenly over the bread layers, pressing down to ensure most of the bread is moistened. Wrap the dish tightly in plastic wrap and refrigerate for at least an hour, or up to 24 hours.

5. When ready to bake, remove the dish from the fridge and allow to stand at room temperature for about 30 minutes. Preheat oven to 190°C (170°C fan-forced).

6. Remove the plastic wrap and scatter the rest of the cheese evenly over the top. Bake until the pudding is light golden-brown and puffy, and the edges have pulled away slightly from the sides of the dish (45–50 minutes). If the pudding looks as though it is over-browning, cover it loosely with baking paper or foil.

7. Cool on a wire rack for a few minutes before sprinkling the remaining chives on top. Serve immediately.

Home-style fried eggs with chilli sauce

Easy
Vegetarian
Dairy-free
⏱ **1–2 hours**
Serves 2–4

We go through dozens and dozens of eggs each week at Billy Kwong, cooking our "staples", which include fried rice and a version of this dish. Although these fried eggs are extremely simple to make, the deliciousness of this recipe relies upon super-fresh eggs. This dish is all about colour and texture for me. What you want is crunchy eggwhites, and crispy golden brown, yet runny, yolks. Serve this dish with some steamed rice, and call it a meal.

2 tbsp chilli sauce (see
    recipe below)
1 cup vegetable oil
4 free-range eggs*
1 tbsp light soy sauce**
pinch of ground white pepper
½ cup spring onions, finely sliced

Chilli sauce (makes 240g or 1 cup)
8 large red chillies, roughly
    chopped
75g ginger, roughly chopped
125ml vegetable oil
1 tsp white sugar
1 tbsp light soy sauce**

* Weekly farmers markets always
  have great free-range or organic
  eggs on offer. Sure, the eggs may
  cost a bit more by the dozen, but
  in my view, it is a worthwhile
  investment, from a sustainability
  and flavour perspective.

** Check soy sauce is gluten-free
   if required

1. **To make the chilli sauce,** chop chilli and ginger in a food processor until finely chopped.

2. Heat oil in a wok until the surface seems to shimmer slightly. Reduce heat to low-medium, add chilli and ginger and cook, stirring regularly, for about 3 minutes to cook out the flavours. Add sugar and cook for one minute, stirring regularly so sauce doesn't catch on the wok base.

3. Stir through soy sauce, reduce heat to low and cook, still stirring, for 10 minutes – the sauce should darken, and the oil will separate. The chilli sauce can be used immediately or cooled and stored in an airtight container in the refrigerator for up to a week.

4. Heat the oil in a hot wok until surface seems to shimmer slightly.

5. Crack eggs into a small bowl, then pour into hot oil. After one minute, reduce heat to medium, allowing the underside of the eggs to become firm and crisp – the yolks should still be runny.

6. Carefully slide a spatula under the eggs, then pour off and discard the oil. Return eggs to wok and cook for a further minute to become crisp.

7. Gently remove eggs from wok and drain off any excess oil before easing onto a plate. Drizzle eggs with soy sauce, chilli sauce, garnish with pepper and spring onions, and serve immediately.

Fish and seafood

Sri Lankan prawn curry with coconut pol sambol

Gluten-free
Dairy-free
🕐 **30 mins–1 hour**
Serves 4

20 large raw king prawns, peeled
    with tails left on, deveined
1 bunch snake beans, cut into
    7cm pieces

Sri Lankan fish curry powder
1 tsp black peppercorns
1 tsp cumin seeds
1 tsp fennel seeds
1 tsp coriander seeds
1 tsp fenugreek seeds
1 cinnamon stick
1 tsp dill seeds
1 tsp ground turmeric

Pol sambol
1 cup desiccated coconut
1 cup coconut milk
½ tsp black peppercorns
1 tbsp Maldive fish flakes
    (available from Sri Lankan and
    Indian food stores)
½ small red onion, finely diced
½ tsp chilli powder
½ tsp smoked hot paprika
juice of 1 lime
1 tsp sea salt

Sri Lankan curry sauce
20ml vegetable oil
1 small brown onion, finely diced
1 tsp sea salt
4 cloves garlic, thinly sliced
1 small green chilli, halved
    lengthways, then thinly sliced
1 stem lemongrass, finely sliced
2 tbsp Sri Lankan fish curry powder
    (see above)
1 sprig fresh curry leaves, leaves
    picked, plus extra sprigs to serve
    (optional)
1 tbsp tamarind puree
250ml coconut cream
juice of 1 lime
steamed rice, to serve

Any seafood rocks in this curry but the flavours also work well with chicken. That requires a little more cooking: use thigh, as it's much more succulent than breast in these circumstances, and yes, preferably skin-on. All the flavour is in the skin.

1. **For the Sri Lankan fish curry powder,** lightly toast the whole spices and grind to a fine powder, then add the turmeric.

2. **For the coconut pol sambol,** soak the desiccated coconut in the coconut milk for 30 minutes. Using a mortar and pestle, finely grind the peppercorns and Maldive fish flakes to a fine powder. Mix all the ingredients together, adding lime juice a little at a time until flavour is balanced. Set aside.

3. **For the Sri Lankan curry sauce,** heat the oil in a heavy-based saucepan over medium heat. Add the onion and salt and cook for about 5 minutes until softened, then add the garlic and chilli and cook for a further 5 minutes. Add the lemongrass and fish curry powder and cook for another 5 minutes. Add the curry leaves, tamarind puree and coconut cream, and cook for 2 minutes.

4. Add prawns and snake beans. Bring to just below the boil and cook for about 2–3 minutes, stirring often. Add a tablespoon or two of water if needed. Remove from heat, cover and stand for 5 minutes, then season to taste and add the remaining lime juice if needed, plus extra curry sprigs if using.

5. Top curry with sambol and serve with rice.

Crispy king prawns with sweet and salty garlic sauce

Easy
Dairy-free
⏱ **less than 30 mins**
Serves 4–6

16 uncooked king prawns,
    about 800g
3 tsp cornflour
2 tsp water
2 tsp light soy sauce
1 egg yolk, lightly beaten
1 tsp sesame oil
vegetable oil, for deep-frying

Sweet and salty garlic sauce
2 tbsp honey
2 tbsp shaoxing wine, or dry sherry
5 tsp light soy sauce
2 cloves garlic, finely diced

This dish relies on the freshest-quality seafood, and, for the sauce, I always try to buy fresh, Australian-grown garlic rather than the lower-quality imported product, which I find leaves too strong an artificial garlicky taste and smell, well after the meal is over. Make sure your deep-frying oil is clean and at the right temperature. Freeze the prawn heads and reserve for stock.

1. Peel, devein and butterfly prawns, leaving tails intact (see step-by-step guide below).

2. Blend cornflour with water in a medium-sized bowl until dissolved. Add prawns, soy sauce, egg yolk and sesame oil and mix well.

3. **For the sweet and salty garlic sauce,** combine ingredients in a small bowl and set aside.

4. Heat oil in a hot wok until surface seems to shimmer slightly. Deep-fry half the prawns over a high heat for one minute. Remove from wok using a slotted spoon and drain on kitchen paper. Repeat process with remaining prawns and set aside.

5. Carefully drain hot oil from wok and wipe clean. Heat the same wok to moderately hot, add reserved sauce ingredients and simmer for 1½ minutes. Lastly, add reserved prawns and stir-fry for a further 30 seconds or until prawns are hot and just cooked through.

6. Arrange prawns on a platter and serve immediately.

How to peel, devein and butterfly prawns

1. Remove head from prawn with a slight twisting motion.

2. Peel shells and legs from body of prawn, leaving tails intact.

3. Lay prawn flat on its side and make an incision down its back.

4. Using the tip of your knife scrape away the dark "vein" and any innards.

5. Prawns are now butterflied, ready for stir-frying or steaming; butterflied prawns cook more quickly and evenly.

Spanner crab omelette with herbs and pickled daikon

Dairy-free
🕐 **1–2 hours**
Serves 2–4

200g (1 cup) picked fresh spanner crabmeat
2 red shallots, halved and thinly sliced
½ bunch mint, leaves picked
½ bunch dill, leaves picked
½ bunch coriander, leaves picked
2 tsp malt vinegar
6 free-range eggs
2 tbsp vegetable oil

Pickled daikon (white radish)
250g daikon (about ⅓ small one)
1 tsp salt flakes
1 tsp white sugar

This simple dish relies on fresh, high-quality free-range or organic eggs and super-fresh Australian crabmeat. I lightly pickle the daikon to add depth to the filling and the picked herbs give the dish an overall lightness, freshness and aroma. For a more cost-effective option, substitute cooked, peeled and chopped local prawns for the crabmeat. Or replace the seafood with beansprouts, pickled carrot shreds, julienned zucchini and snowpeas and your favourite fresh herbs.

1. **To make the pickled daikon**, peel and slice the daikon into thin rounds, then julienne. Place the daikon, salt and sugar in a small bowl and combine well with your hands. Refrigerate for 1 hour. Drain liquid from daikon, squeezing to remove any excess liquid.

2. Combine pickled daikon with crabmeat, shallot, herbs and vinegar and toss with your hands to distribute ingredients evenly.

3. Crack eggs into a large bowl and beat lightly with a fork until just combined.

4. Heat oil in a wok or 28cm non-stick frying pan until the surface seems to shimmer slightly. Pour in beaten egg and leave to cook, without stirring on the base of the wok or pan, for 30 seconds.

5. Using a spatula, flip the egg over and leave to cook for another 30 seconds.

6. Add crabmeat filling to the centre of the omelette, then using a spatula, fold omelette over and leave for 20 seconds, before lifting omelette onto a serving platter. Serve immediately.

Chilli salt and pepper squid with fresh lime

Egg-free
🕐 **less than 30 mins**
Serves 4

500g squid
1 ½ tbsp cornflour
1 ½ tbsp plain flour
2 tsp sea salt
1 tsp chilli powder
1 tsp crushed Sichuan peppercorns
vegetable oil, for deep-frying
4 small iceberg lettuce leaves, chilled
2 limes, halved
handful coriander sprigs
handful mint leaves

This dish is obviously best cooked "a la minute" so make sure you have all of your ingredients prepared, your serving plate with lettuce cups and fresh herbs ready to go, and your guests seated before you begin frying the squid. It only takes a few minutes to cook and is so delicious eaten piping hot.

1. First, clean and score the squid (see step-by-step guide below).

2. In a large bowl, combine flours, salt, chilli powder and Sichuan pepper. Add squid and toss to coat, shaking off any excess flour.

3. Heat oil in a hot wok until surface seems to shimmer slightly. Add half the squid and deep-fry for about 1½ minutes or until just tender and beginning to colour. Remove with a slotted spoon and drain well on paper towel. Repeat process with remaining squid.

4. Arrange chilled lettuce cups on a platter and top with squid. Serve immediately with lime halves and fresh herbs.

How to clean and score squid

1. Gently pull the head and tentacles away from the body and discard the entrails.

2. Cut the tentacles from the head just below the eyes. Reserve the tentacles and discard the head.

3. Remove and discard the fine, purplish-black membrane from the body.

4. Trim the side "wings" from the body and set aside.

5. Pull out the clear "backbone" (quill) from inside the body, then rinse body, tentacles and wings thoroughly and pat dry with kitchen paper.

6. Cut squid down the centre so that it will open out flat.

7. Using a sharp knife, score shallow diagonal cuts in a crisscross pattern on the inside surface, taking care not to cut right through the squid. Scoring squid makes it curl on contact with hot oil, while also allowing flavours to penetrate into the squid.

8. Cut the scored squid in half and then into 4cm strips.

9. Trim the reserved "wings", then cut in half.

Fish and seafood

Braised octopus with potatoes

Easy
Egg-free
🕐 **1–2 hours**
Serves 4

1 x 600g octopus, fresh or thawed
   out from frozen
2 celery sticks, thinly sliced
1 small red onion, peeled and
   kept whole
1 fresh bird's eye chilli
½ bunch flat-leaf parsley, leaves
   picked, stalks reserved
zest and juice of 1 lemon
600g small pink-eye or kipfler
   potatoes, peeled
sea salt and freshly ground black
   pepper, to season
extra virgin olive oil
2 tbsp salted capers, rinsed

This is a nice, simple Italian-style dish – the octopus can easily be replaced by squid or even prawns. The oil and potatoes work so well with seafood.

1. Rinse octopus under cold running water. Place the whole octopus into a medium thick-bottomed pan and add the celery, onion, chilli, parsley stalks and lemon zest.

2. Cover with cold water and bring to the boil, then reduce heat to a very low simmer and cook, half covered, for 1 hour or until soft. Remove from heat and leave the octopus to cool in the liquid, uncovered.

3. Bring a large pan of salted water to the boil. Add potatoes and cook for 20 minutes, until cooked but still quite firm, then drain and cut into rough 2cm cubes. Put potatoes into a bowl, season with sea salt and black pepper, and drizzle with olive oil. Chop parsley leaves and add to potatoes. Lightly toss together and set aside.

4. When the octopus has cooled, remove from the cooking liquid and cut into 3-4cm pieces. Place octopus into a bowl, add the lemon juice, 3 tablespoons of olive oil and the capers. Season with sea salt and black pepper and toss.

5. Serve potato salad with the octopus at room temperature.

Fish and seafood

Salmon with coconut milk, glass noodles and herbs

Easy
Dairy-free
🕐 **less than 30 mins**
Serves 4

This brilliant one-pot dish really couldn't get any easier. Just throw everything in together and it's all done in a matter of minutes. Simple!

400ml can coconut milk
2 tbsp fish sauce
2 tsp sugar
juice of 1 lime
1 small brown onion, finely sliced
3 cloves garlic, crushed
1 large red chilli, sliced
4 small salmon fillets (around 150g
   each), skin removed
200g dried mung bean vermicelli
   (glass noodles)
½ cup each of loosely packed basil,
   mint and coriander

1. Place coconut milk, fish sauce, sugar, lime juice, onion, garlic and chilli in a frying pan, covered, and bring to a simmer with a ½ cup of water.

2. Add salmon and reduce heat to low. Cover with the lid and poach for 5 minutes.

3. Add noodles around the salmon and replace the cover to allow the noodles to absorb the liquid. Cook for a further 5 minutes.

4. Stir through most of the herbs and serve immediately with the remaining herbs scattered on top.

ADAM LIAW

Tuna and avocado sushi salad

Easy
Dairy-free
🕐 **less than 30 mins**
Serves 4

400g tuna steaks
1 tsp vegetable oil
200g mixed baby leaves
1 Lebanese cucumber, peeled, sliced
1 cup mixed cherry tomatoes, halved
4 spring onions, finely sliced
2 ripe avocados, sliced
2 tbsp toasted black and white
    sesame seeds
1 sheet nori

Soy and sesame dressing
1 tsp caster sugar
1 tsp soy sauce
2 tsp sesame oil
2 tsp extra virgin olive oil
2 tsp rice vinegar

Sushi without rice, in salad form – genius! I always make sure a salad dressing contains a salty or savoury ingredient, such as a lug of soy sauce or fish sauce, or a good pinch of salt. The oil in the dressing will help stop the salt from wilting the leaves.

1. **For the dressing,** whisk together the ingredients. Set aside.

2. Cut the tuna steaks into 5cm-wide strips. Heat a frying pan over medium heat until hot, then add the oil. Season the tuna well with salt and pepper and fry on all sides for 30 seconds a side. Set aside to cool slightly, then slice into ½ cm strips.

3. Toss together leaves, cucumber, tomatoes and spring onions. Top with the avocado, tuna and sesame seeds. Wave the nori over an open gas flame for a few seconds until it becomes brittle, then crumble over the salad. Serve with the dressing on the side.

Fish and seafood

goodfood

Pan-fried swordfish with celeriac puree and herb salad

Fish cooked in brown butter is superb – and so easy. Add a little oil to the butter so it is less likely to burn, flavour with herbs and baste as you go for a delicious, moist result. This is a great method for cooking chicken, too.

⏱ 30 mins–1 hour
Serves 4

4 x 200g skinless swordfish steaks
sea salt
100ml olive oil
60g butter
½ bunch thyme
lemon wedges, to serve

Celeriac puree
300g celeriac, peeled,
   roughly chopped
200g pink-eye potatoes, peeled,
   roughly chopped
1 Granny Smith apple, peeled,
   roughly chopped
100ml extra virgin olive oil
1 tbsp lemon juice
sea salt and black pepper

Herb salad
80g mache (lamb's tongue lettuce),
   baby kale or baby spinach
½ bunch mint
½ bunch tarragon
½ bunch coriander
2 tbsp extra virgin olive oil
3 tsp lemon juice
sea salt and pepper

1. **To make the celeriac puree,** place celeriac and potato in a steamer over simmering water and steam for 20 minutes. Add apple and steam for a further 10 minutes. Remove when they are soft. Pass the celeriac, potato and apples through a food mill, or press through a sieve. Place in a bowl and slowly stir in the extra virgin olive oil, lemon juice, salt and pepper. Keep warm.

2. **To make the herb salad,** pick and wash the salad leaves and herbs, spin dry or dry on a tea towel. Combine and refrigerate. To make a dressing for the salad, mix the extra virgin olive oil and the lemon juice together, season and stir. Set aside.

3. Season fish to taste. Place a heavy cast-iron pan large enough to fit the 4 steaks on medium heat. Add oil, butter and thyme. As soon as this starts to foam, add the fish and cook, spooning the foaming butter over the fish occasionally. Cook for about 4 minutes, until golden brown. Turn, cooking for a further 4 minutes until golden brown. Cook a little longer if you don't want the fish medium-rare.

4. Place the salad leaves in a serving bowl and add the dressing.

5. Spoon celeriac puree onto four plates, top with swordfish, then spoon the thyme-flavoured burnt butter over the fish and garnish with the thyme sprigs. Serve with the herb salad and lemon wedges.

Cuban fish sandwiches

🕐 **30 mins–1 hour**
Serves 4

4 whole small fish, about
  100g–150g (butterflied, bones
  removed but tail on)
2 eggs
150g plain flour
250g breadcrumbs (dried or fresh)
500ml canola oil, for frying
4 soft bread rolls
1 head iceberg lettuce
1 small white onion, diced
homemade fries, to serve

Soffrito mayonnaise
3 tbsp olive oil
1 small onion, finely diced
1 small green capsicum,
  finely diced
1 small red capsicum, finely diced
1 long red chilli, finely diced
  (optional)
3 cloves garlic, finely minced
250ml tomato passata
125ml dry white wine
250g mayonnaise
1 lime, for squeezing
Tabasco, to taste (optional)

Cuba's best-known claim to food fame is the Cubano,
a toasted sandwich filled with roast pork, glazed ham, swiss
cheese and dill pickles. But this fish sandwich also deserves
a share of the spotlight. The best Cuban fish sandwich is sold
at a place in Miami called La Camaronera, where you eat
standing elbow to elbow at the counter. For true authenticity,
look for a fish small enough to fit whole inside the bun, and
serve it butterflied, bones removed but the tail left on.

1. To make the soffrito mayonnaise, heat the oil in a medium saute
   pan over medium heat. Add onion, capsicum, chilli and garlic with
   a pinch of salt and cook until soft and translucent. Add passata
   and the white wine and simmer gently over low heat for about
   10–15 minutes until everything comes together and is reduced by
   half. Season with salt to taste and set aside to cool.

2. When cool, mix the soffrito with the mayonnaise, a squeeze of
   lime and a few dashes of Tabasco and keep in the fridge. This
   makes more than you need for the sandwiches but it will keep
   for a couple of weeks in the fridge. (It's a delicious dipping
   sauce for cooked prawns or potato croquettes.)

3. Season the fillets with salt and let them sit for a few minutes to
   allow that to sink in. Set up 3 bowls or deep plates with flour in
   one, the whisked eggs in another and breadcrumbs in the last, and
   a flat plate at the end of your assembly line. Coat the fish in flour,
   then drag through the egg and finally coat in the breadcrumbs and
   set aside. Repeat with the remaining fish.

4. Heat about 2cm of canola oil in a large saute pan over medium-high
   heat. When the oil reaches 180°C–190°C on a thermometer, add
   fish to the pan. (If you don't have a thermometer, you'll know it's the
   right temperature if the oil bubbles rapidly when you add the fish. If
   it doesn't, take the fish out and let the oil get hotter.) When the fish
   is golden-brown, flip it and cook the other side. Remove from the
   pan, drain on a paper towel and immediately sprinkle with some salt.

5. Split buns in half and place the fish on the bottom half of each
   bun. Top with iceberg lettuce, some finely chopped onions and a
   good spoonful of soffrito mayonnaise. Add the top of the bun and
   serve with homemade fries.

◆ **Tip** Try to find a soft white sandwich roll that has a thin, crisp crust and
   tender crumb. Something chewy like a baguette simply will not be right.
   As for the fish, choose something flaky, thin and tender like a sand whiting
   or red spot whiting, or a small, skinned snapper or flathead.

Fish and seafood

ANDREW
McCONNELL

Steamed whole fish with soy, ginger and spring onion

Served whole at a Lunar New Year banquet, this steamed fish represents family and prosperity.

Dairy-free
🕐 **30 mins–1 hour**
Serves 4

1 whole snapper (about 1.2kg)
80g young fresh ginger, peeled and finely sliced
½ bunch spring onion, finely sliced, green section only
120ml grapeseed oil
50ml light soy sauce
50ml sweet ginger vinegar*
1 tbsp lemon juice
sea salt and white pepper
½ bunch coriander, leaves picked and washed
½ bunch chrysanthemum, leaves picked and washed (optional)

*Sweet ginger vinegar is available at Asian and speciality grocers.

1. Clean the snapper of any stray scales and pat dry inside and out with paper towel. Using a sharp knife, score the flesh on both sides of the fish, gently making incisions about 1cm-deep across the fish. Season both sides with a little salt. Arrange the prepared fish on a piece of lightly oiled baking paper and place in your steamer basket. Top the fish with the ginger and spring onion.

2. Meanwhile, fill a large saucepan with about 2cm water and bring it to a boil. When ready, place the steamer over the water, top with the lid and cook, covered, for about 20 minutes or until the fish flakes easily when tested with a fork in the thickest part. I start checking this from time to time around the 10-minute mark.

3. Meanwhile, make the dressing by mixing together the oil, soy, sweet ginger vinegar and lemon juice. Season with salt and white pepper to taste.

4. When the fish is ready, remove from the steamer and carefully transfer the whole fish onto a large serving platter. Season the fish with a little salt and douse quite liberally with the dressing. Scatter the coriander and chrysanthemum leaves over the fish to serve.

goodfood

Chicken, duck and meat

Chicken and pickled ginger in honey sauce

This classic Asian dish provides maximum flavour for minimum effort – perfect for those weeknights when time is of the essence.

Easy
🕐 **less than 30 mins**
Serves 2

4 free-range or organic chicken legs, chopped through the bone into bite-sized pieces
peanut oil, for deep-frying
125g pickled ginger, finely sliced
1 red capsicum, roughly chopped
1 green capsicum, roughly chopped
1 tsp shaoxing wine
2 tbsp honey
1 tbsp dark soy sauce
1 tsp sea salt
250ml fresh chicken stock
coriander leaves, steamed rice and greens, to serve

For the marinade
1 tbsp light soy sauce
1 tsp dark soy sauce
1 tsp shaoxing wine
½ tsp salt

1. To make the marinade, combine soy sauces, shaoxing wine and salt. Add the chicken pieces and leave for 30 minutes.

2. Heat peanut oil in a wok or deep fryer until just smoking (180°C), and deep-fry the chicken in batches until lightly browned (1-2 minutes per batch). Remove and drain on paper towel. Pour all but 2 tablespoons of oil from the wok.

3. Reheat the wok until just smoking. Add ginger and capsicum and stir-fry for 30 seconds until fragrant, then deglaze the wok with the shaoxing wine.

4. Return chicken to the wok, then add honey, dark soy sauce, sea salt and chicken stock. Cover and simmer over medium heat for 3 minutes, or until chicken is cooked through. Garnish with coriander leaves, and serve with steamed rice and greens in oyster sauce.

Butterflied roast chicken with gluten-free ricotta, garlic and spice stuffing

Gluten-free
🕐 **2 hours +**
Serves 4

2kg free-range chicken
extra virgin olive oil
sea salt
freshly ground black pepper

For the stuffing
4 cloves garlic, finely chopped
sea salt
½ Spanish onion, finely chopped
125g unsalted butter, chopped,
    at room temperature
1 tsp coriander seeds, roasted and
    lightly crushed
1 tsp cumin seeds roasted and
    lightly crushed
2 tbsp finely chopped flat-leaf
    parsley
2 tbsp finely chopped chives
125g ricotta
juice of 1 lemon
freshly ground black pepper

The technique of stuffing the chicken under the skin adds extra deliciousness. This dish is perfect with roast potatoes and a green salad. And if you buy a quality free-range or organic chook, I promise you will taste the difference.

1. **To make the stuffing,** put the garlic and a large pinch of sea salt in a mortar and pound with the pestle until a paste forms. Add the onion and crush slightly, then the butter and spices. Mix through, then add the herbs and ricotta. Add lemon juice and a large pinch of both sea salt and freshly ground black pepper.

2. Remove the chicken from refrigerator 2 hours before cooking and bring to room temperature. To butterfly the chicken, cut down each side of the backbone and push down gently but firmly on the breastplate. Remove the wishbone, then slide a hand between the skin and flesh to gently loosen the skin.

3. Take some stuffing in your hand and put it under the skin of each leg, a little at a time, until the pocket is full and even. Repeat the process with the skin on top of the chicken breasts. Smooth the skin out and you should have a very handsome bird sitting in front of you, all puffed up and shiny.

4. Preheat oven to 160°C. Rub the skin with extra virgin olive oil and season all over with sea salt. Put the chicken in a roasting tin and cook for 45 minutes, then turn the heat up to 180°C for 15 minutes to get some colour on the skin. Remove the tin from the oven, drain off the juices and put them to one side. Cover the chicken with foil and rest for 30 minutes.

5. Place the chicken on a chopping board, cut down the middle, then remove the legs. Cut each leg into thighs and drumsticks, and each breast into two. Put the chicken pieces on plates and spoon the reserved juices from the roasting tray over the top. Add a generous grind of black pepper and serve.

Sticky ginger roast chicken

⏱ **2 hours +**
Serves 4

The key to this sticky chicken is getting the glaze to caramelise under the grill. A bit of charring is good, but keep an eye on it as you don't want it to burn.

1.7kg whole free-range chicken
2 tbsp olive oil
1 tbsp brown sugar
1 tsp sea salt
1 tbsp smoked paprika
1 tsp ground cumin

Ginger barbecue sauce
¾ cup tomato sauce
1 tbsp butter
1 tbsp grated ginger
1 tbsp soy sauce
1 tbsp Worcestershire sauce
2 tbsp malt vinegar
1 tbsp honey
1 tbsp Dijon mustard

1. With poultry shears or a heavy knife, remove the backbone of the chicken and press on the breastbone to flatten the bird. Chop the backbone into pieces and make one cut through to the bone at the meatiest part of each drumstick. Rub both sides of the bird with oil, brown sugar, salt, paprika and cumin and allow to stand for 40 minutes.

2. Preheat oven to 120°C. Place the backbone in the base of a roasting tin and place the chicken on top. Roast for 2 hours, basting occasionally. Remove the bird from the oven to rest and increase the heat to 200°C on a grill setting, or by simply setting your grill to high.

3. While the chicken is resting, combine the ingredients for the ginger barbecue sauce in a small saucepan and stir over medium heat until the butter is melted and the honey dissolved. Add a few tablespoons of the resting juices from the chicken if there are any. Brush the chicken well with the barbecue sauce and return to the oven under the grill for 5–10 minutes until the sauce is sticky and caramelised. Serve immediately.

◆ **Tip** "Butterflying" a whole chicken allows you to crisp more of the skin while also helping the bird to cook a bit faster. The chopped backbone in the pan acts as a trivet, allowing air to circulate under the chicken while adding great flavour to any pan sauces.

Steamed chicken with asparagus and fennel

Make the most of that steamer sitting forgotten in the cupboard with this wholesome plate of greens and steamed chicken breasts.

Easy
Gluten-free
🕐 **30 mins–1 hour**
Serves 4

4 skinless chicken breasts
2 bunches asparagus, trimmed
2 bunches broccolini, trimmed
100g peas
1 fennel, trimmed
1 spring onion, finely chopped
3 tbsp extra virgin olive oil
2 tbsp lemon juice
sea salt and freshly ground
    black pepper

Spring onion sauce
3 spring onions, chopped
2 tbsp garlic aioli or whole
    egg mayo
2 tbsp plain yoghurt

1. Set up a two-level steamer with boiling water. Season the chicken well with salt and pepper and place in a shallow heatproof bowl. Steam the chicken for 10-12 minutes or until just cooked through, then set aside to rest for 2 minutes. Steam the asparagus and broccolini for 4 minutes and the peas (in a small heatproof bowl) for 2 minutes, then drain.

2. Finely shave the fennel crosswise and toss with chopped spring onion, olive oil, lemon juice, sea salt and pepper.

3. Whiz the sauce ingredients in a food processor until smooth and season well. Thickly slice chicken against the grain. Toss vegetables with the fennel mixture, then slice asparagus and broccolini in half and transfer to serving plates with the peas. Arrange chicken and spring onion sauce on top, add the fennel, drizzle with any leftover dressing and serve.

goodfood

Chicken and capsicum tray bake

Easy
Gluten-free
🕐 **30 mins–1 hour**
Serves 4–6

2 tbsp olive oil
6 chicken thigh cutlets, bone-in
salt and pepper, to season
2 red onions, peeled and cut
    into wedges
4 cloves garlic, peeled and lightly
    crushed
1 red capsicum, cut into thick slices
1 yellow capsicum, cut into
    thick slices
6 anchovies, chopped (optional)
½ cup chicken stock
a pinch of sugar
1 cup loosely packed basil
    leaves, torn
splash of balsamic vinegar
    (optional)

This simple summery bake is an easy dinner that combines the natural affinity of basil and capsicum with succulent roast chicken.

1. Preheat oven to 200°C. Heat a large flameproof, ovenproof baking dish or frying pan over high heat. Add oil, season the chicken with salt and pepper and cook, skin-side down, until golden brown.

2. Turn the chicken and add the onions, garlic and capsicum around the chicken pieces. Scatter with the anchovies (if using) and pour over the stock. Season very well with salt, pepper and a good pinch of sugar, transfer to the oven and cook for 30–35 minutes or until the chicken is just cooked though.

3. Scatter with basil and serve immediately, with a splash of balsamic vinegar on top if you like.

Chicken, duck and meat

Parsi-braised chicken marylands

Gluten-free
⏱ **2 hours +**
Serves 4

Adapted from traditional Persian curries, this aromatic dish is the kind of thing I crave when it's cold and I want to cook at home. Paired with a beautiful rice pilaf and citrus-roasted carrots, you've taken what could be a yummy weeknight dinner and turned it into a meal you could easily and impressively entertain with.

60g cloves garlic, peeled
60g ginger, peeled
4 large chicken marylands
400g sliced onion
85g butter
2 tbsp olive oil
8 cardamon pods
6 whole cloves
2 sprigs curry leaves
2 tsp black mustard seeds
1 cinnamon quill
5 small dried red chillies
2 dried guajillo chillies*
100ml white wine
1 tin crushed tomatoes
2 tbsp jaggery or brown sugar
salt
basmati rice and yoghurt, to serve

*Even though guajillos are, in fact, a Mexican variety of chilli, I use them in all kinds of dishes. Their heat is quite warming and gently builds in the background, unlike some dried Asian varieties, which hit you with heat from the first bite. They are worth seeking out and adding to a variety of soups and stews. Guajillo chillies are available from specialist suppliers such as Fireworks Foods, The Essential Ingredient and Herbie's Spices.

1. Using a mortar and pestle, a blender or a microplane, puree the ginger and garlic into a paste with a pinch of salt. Mix and set aside. This will make more than you need but the mixture will keep in the fridge for a few days.

2. Season the chicken with salt and rub with some of the ginger-garlic paste. Leave the chicken to marinate in the fridge for 1 hour.

3. Set a wide pan over medium-high heat and add the butter and olive oil. Add the chicken, skin-side down, and cook for a few minutes to brown a bit of the skin without burning the ginger-garlic paste (a bit of caramelisation is totally fine as long as it doesn't go into burnt territory).

4. Remove the chicken from the pan and set aside. Immediately add the onions and cook until they are softened and starting to caramelise. Then add the cardamom, cloves, curry leaves, mustard seeds, cinnamon and chillies. Sizzle together until very aromatic.

5. Add white wine and cook for a minute. Add crushed tomatoes, the jaggery and 1 litre of cold water. Return the chicken to the pan, in one even layer, and bring to a simmer. Reduce heat to low and cook for 45 minutes–1 hour with a lid slightly ajar or with a baking paper lid (cartouche). Every now and then, flip the chicken pieces over so every bit of it has some time cooking in the sauce. To know when the chicken is cooked, wiggle the thigh. It will start to feel loose in the joint. You may need to add more water if you cook it much longer.

6. When the chicken is meltingly tender, it's ready to serve. Serve with basmati rice or a simple pilaf and a dollop of yoghurt.

Chicken, duck and meat

Japanese-style chicken meatballs

Easy
⊙ **30 mins**
Serves 4

400g skinless chicken thighs,
    minced
2 spring onions, finely sliced
1cm ginger, peeled and finely
    grated
2 tsp soy sauce
2 tsp mirin
½ tsp sesame oil
3 tsp whisked egg
1-2 tsp cornflour vegetable oil,
    for frying
coriander leaves, to serve

Sauce
2½ tsp soy sauce
2½ tbsp mirin
½ tbsp caster sugar
1 tbsp hoisin sauce
1 clove garlic, crushed

These meatballs make the perfect starter or main for a fresh, zesty Asian inspired meal.

1. **To make the sauce**, combine ingredients in a bowl and whisk together.

2. **To make the meatballs**, place the chicken, spring onion and ginger in another large bowl and combine until smooth and completely incorporated. Add soy sauce, mirin, sesame oil, egg and cornflour and mix well, adding extra cornflour if needed – the mixture is meant to be quite soft. With moistened hands, roll it into small balls about 4cm in diameter.

3. Pour 2cm vegetable oil into a frying pan and heat to about 180°C. Add the meatballs in batches, taking care not to crowd the pan, and cook for 3–5 minutes until browned on all sides and cooked through. Remove the balls and drain the oil into a heatproof container, wipe the pan with kitchen paper and return to high heat. Add the sauce and cook for 2–3 minutes until smooth and thick. Add the balls and coat with the sauce.

4. Spoon meatballs onto a large plate and sprinkle with coriander.

goodfood

Chicken, duck and meat

NEIL PERRY

Middle-Eastern braised chicken with green olives

For this recipe, try to source quality free-range chicken, if possible. The flavour will be great and well worth the effort – and, ideally, you won't need to use chicken stock. Serve with a simple fennel and orange salad and cous cous or rice.

Easy
Gluten-free
⏱ **30 mins–1 hour**
Serves 4

60ml extra virgin olive oil,
    plus extra 3 tbsp
8 free-range chicken thighs,
    bone-in, skin on
1½ tsp sea salt
1 tbsp finely chopped garlic
1 tsp ground ginger
1 tsp freshly ground black pepper
½ tsp ground cumin
½ tsp sweet paprika
30g Italian parsley leaves, chopped
30g coriander leaves, chopped
2 pinches saffron, steeped in 30ml
    boiling water
2 large red onions, peeled, halved
    and sliced thinly
500ml boiling water (or chicken
    stock if you prefer a deeper
    chicken flavour)
400g large green olives, pitted
juice of 2 lemons
coriander, to garnish

1. Heat half the oil in a casserole dish over medium-high heat. Sprinkle the chicken thighs with 1 teaspoon of the salt and, in 2 batches, cook for about 7 minutes (adding a bit more oil for second batch, if necessary) until skin is browned. Remove chicken and set aside. Discard all oil and wipe out pan.

2. Using a mortar and pestle or a blender, combine garlic, ginger, pepper, cumin, paprika, parsley, coriander, remaining ½ teaspoon salt, 3 tablespoons extra virgin olive oil and saffron water to form a paste.

3. Place remaining 30ml olive oil in the casserole dish over a medium heat. Add onion and spice paste and cook, stirring regularly, for 5-10 minutes, until onion becomes translucent. Stir in the chicken thighs to coat in the spice mix. Continue stirring while slowly adding the boiling water or chicken stock. Reduce heat to a gentle simmer, cover the casserole and cook for 30 minutes.

4. Add olives, cover and cook for a further 10 minutes, then stir in the lemon juice. Remove from heat and rest, uncovered, for five minutes. At this stage, you can remove the chicken and reduce the sauce if it's a little too watery.

5. Place chicken on plates, spoon over olives and sauce, garnish with coriander and serve.

Crisp-skinned duck, lentil, broccoli and walnut salad

Easy
Gluten-free
🕐 **30 mins–1 hour**
Serves 4

300g raw lentils, rinsed
1 red onion, halved and finely sliced
4 duck breasts
sea salt and cracked black pepper,
    to taste
150g broccoli florets
handful wild rocket or baby
    spinach leaves
lebanese cucumber, cut into
    small chunks
2 or 3 pink radishes, finely sliced
2 tbsp walnuts, toasted
1 tsp poppy seeds

For the dressing
2 tbsp extra virgin olive oil
2 tbsp red wine or sherry vinegar
1 tbsp honey

Summer eating should be easy-going and relaxed – food you can cook in advance, then eat at room temperature. Seared duck breast is sliced and served – pink and tender – with a chilled-out salad of lentils, broccoli, radish and walnuts speckled with poppy seeds.

1. Combine lentils, half the onion and 1 litre water in a medium saucepan and bring to the boil. Simmer gently for 25-30 minutes, until lentils are tender. Drain.

2. Using a sharp knife, score the skin of the duck in a criss-cross pattern. Rub sea salt and pepper into the skin and set aside.

3. Cook the duck, skin-side down, in a dry pan over low heat for 10 minutes, until the fat melts and the skin is crisp. Pour off the fat (cool and refrigerate for future use), turn the breasts and cook for five minutes or until just firm to the touch. Set aside to rest.

4. Pulse broccoli in a food processor to break up. Whisk the dressing ingredients together in a large bowl. Add rocket, broccoli, cucumber, radish, walnuts and remaining sliced onion and toss well to combine. Serve with the sliced duck and scatter with poppy seeds to serve.

◆ **Tip** Skip cooking your own lentils if it's too hot, and open a can.

KYLIE KWONG

Spicy salt duck breasts with lemon

Easy
🕐 **30 mins–1 hour**
Serves 4

In our family, duck dishes are usually only offered on special occasions and in my restaurant, the signature dish of almost 17 years has been our deep-fried duck with orange and plum. Many may feel intimidated by cooking a whole duck, so this recipe, using duck breasts, works really well for everyday use. Excellent quality, locally produced duck is available from many farmers' markets. In this recipe, you simply steam the duck breasts then deep-fry for texture.

4 x 200g duck breasts, with skin, trimmed of excess fat
2 tbsp plain flour
2½ tbsp spicy-salt mix (see below)
vegetable oil, for deep-frying
1 large red chilli, finely sliced on the diagonal
2 tbsp spring onion, julienne
handful of coriander sprigs
2 lemons, halved
steamed rice, to serve

Spicy salt (makes 2½ tablespoons)
1 tsp Sichuan peppercorns
1 tsp fennel seeds
1 tsp coriander seeds
1 tsp cumin seeds
2 tbsp salt flakes

1. **To make the spicy salt**, combine all ingredients in a heavy-based frying pan and dry-roast over medium heat, tossing occasionally. When the peppercorns begin to pop and become aromatic, about 1-2 minutes, take off the heat. Allow to cool, then coarsely grind using a mortar and pestle or spice grinder.

2. Arrange duck breasts, skin-side up, on a heatproof plate that will fit inside a steamer basket. Place plate inside steamer, position over a deep saucepan or wok of boiling water and steam, covered for 12 minutes or until duck breasts are half cooked.

3. Meanwhile, in a large bowl, combine flour with spicy salt mixture. Carefully remove plate from steamer basket, transfer duck breasts to a rack and set aside for 25 minutes to cool slightly.

4. Add duck breasts to spicy-salt mixture and toss to coat well, shaking off any excess flour. Heat enough oil to cover duck breasts in a large hot wok until surface seems to shimmer slightly. Add duck and deep fry for about 2 minutes or until just cooked through and lightly browned. Remove and drain well on paper towel.

5. Slice duck diagonally into 1cm slices and arrange on a platter. Garnish with chilli, spring onion, coriander and serve immediately with lemon halves.

Tips
◆ Be sure to cool the duck for the 25 minutes specified in the recipe, so the meat can rest well ensuring juiciness and tenderness.
◆ Store any leftover spicy salt in an airtight container
◆ Use this recipe as a base and swap the spicy salt for your preferred sauce – eg, sweet and sour, or a sweet, syrupy citrus sauce with orange, mandarin or tangelo. Sweet-chilli would be a great dipping sauce.

Chicken, duck and meat

JILL DUPLEIX

Lamb kofta with zucchini noodles

It might look like spaghetti with meatballs, but the spaghetti is zucchini, the meatballs are lamb kofta, and the tomato sauce is spiced up with harissa.

Gluten-free
🕐 **less than 30 mins**
Serves 4

750g lamb shoulder, minced
1 onion, grated
1 tbsp ground cumin
2 tsp ground cinnamon
1 tsp salt
½ tsp ground pepper
1 egg, beaten
2 tbsp olive oil
3 medium-large zucchini
fresh coriander leaves for serving

For the sauce
400g can tomatoes, chopped
400g tomato passata or sugo
200ml stock or water
1 tsp ground cinnamon
1 tsp smoked paprika
1 tsp harissa or chilli sauce
1 tsp sugar

1. To make the kofta, combine the lamb, onion, cumin, cinnamon, salt and pepper in a bowl and knead with your hands until well mixed. Add egg and mix well. Divide into golfball-size portions and roll into balls.

2. Heat oil in a large heavy frying pan over medium heat and cook meatballs, in batches, until well browned. Set aside. In the same pan, combine tomatoes, tomato passata, stock, cinnamon, paprika, harissa, sugar, salt and pepper and bring to the boil, stirring. Simmer gently, stirring occasionally, for 15 minutes.

3. Spiralise the zucchini, or use a vegetable peeler to shave the zucchini lengthwise, then slice each shaving into long strips. Add zucchini to the sauce and cook for 2 minutes until softened, then return the meatballs to the pan and heat through.

4. Scatter with coriander and extra pepper and serve.

goodfood

Spring stir-fry with lamb and spring onions

Easy
🕐 **less than 30 mins**
Serves 4

500g lamb backstrap, cut into
    1½cm pieces
3 tbsp peanut oil
4 spring onions, cut into julienne
2 tbsp light soy sauce
2 tbsp sugar
1 tsp sesame oil
pinch of freshly ground
    white pepper
chilli oil, to serve

Marinade
2 cloves garlic, finely chopped
2 tbsp light soy sauce
2 tbsp shaoxing wine
2 tsp sugar

This succulent lamb stir-fry is easy to prepare. Substitute asparagus for spring onions when in season.

1. To make the marinade, mix together the garlic, soy sauce, shaoxing and sugar.

2. Add lamb to marinade mix, leave for 1 hour, then drain.

3. Heat a wok over high heat until just smoking. Add the peanut oil and, when hot, stir-fry the lamb in batches until well browned, about 2-3 minutes, then remove from the wok.

4. Add spring onions to the wok and stir-fry for 1 minute, then add the soy sauce, sugar, sesame oil, pepper and lamb. Toss to coat the meat with the sauce, then use a slotted spoon to transfer the meat to a serving plate. Simmer the sauce for about 2 minutes until it reduces and thickens. Pour over the lamb and serve with chilli oil.

Chicken, duck and meat

ADAM LIAW

Roast lamb shoulder shawarma

🕐 **2 hours +**
Serves 4

The shawarma seasoning mix listed here makes a double portion. Store the leftovers in a jar or zip-lock bag for lamb chops, stews, or a repeat performance.

1.5kg bone-in lamb shoulder
2 tbsp olive oil
1 brown onion, peeled and cut
   into chunks
4-8 pita breads, to serve
¼ cup toasted pine nuts, to serve
finely shredded parsley, to serve
1 red onion, sliced
1 tomato, sliced
1 cucumber, sliced
3 cups finely shredded lettuce,
   to serve
1 lemon, quartered, to serve
   (optional)

**Shawarma seasoning
(makes double)**
1 tsp ground black pepper
½ tsp ground allspice
2 tsp garlic powder
½ tsp ground cloves
1 tsp ground cinnamon
1 tsp ground cumin
1 tsp ground coriander seed
1 tsp paprika
2 tsp dried oregano
2 tsp salt

Garlic sesame sauce
1 cup yoghurt
2 tbsp tahini
1 tbsp lemon juice
1 tsp honey
2 cloves crushed garlic
½ tsp salt
olive oil, for drizzling

1. Combine shawarma seasoning ingredients. Mix half of the mixture with the oil and rub all over the lamb. Reserve the remaining seasoning for future use. Allow the lamb to marinate in the fridge overnight.

2. Preheat oven to 175°C (155°C fan-forced). Place onion in the base of a lidded pan or roasting tray and top with the lamb. Add 1 cup water to the pan, cover tightly and roast for 4 hours. You can uncover the lamb for the last 30 minutes if you like it well-browned. Wrap the pita bread in foil and place in the oven for the last 20 minutes of cooking to warm through.

3. Remove lamb from the oven, baste with the juices from the pan and rest for 15 minutes. Combine the ingredients for the sauce, finishing with a drizzle of olive oil. Scatter the lamb with parsley and pine nuts and serve with the pitas, fillings, vegetables and sauce.

Chicken, duck and meat

Greek lamb and feta pie

⏱ 2 hours +
Serves 4–6

1 tbsp olive oil
2 red onions, peeled, sliced
5 cloves garlic, finely chopped
1 boneless lamb shoulder
  (about 1.2kg)
½ preserved lemon, sliced
zest of 1 lemon
2 tsp dried oregano
1 cup (250ml) dry white wine
1 cup (250ml) chicken stock
½ cup Persian-style marinated feta

Topping
175g kataifi pastry*, defrosted in
  the fridge
2 tbsp olive oil
Greek basil leaves, to serve
  (optional)

* Frozen kataifi pastry is available
  from gourmet grocers

The light crunch of the golden pastry is the perfect partner to the shredded slow-cooked lamb and background tang of preserved lemon.

1. Preheat oven to 150°C.

2. Place a large ovenproof casserole dish over medium heat. Add the olive oil then the onions and garlic cloves and cook until onions are soft and translucent. Add the lamb and brown on all sides. Add the remaining ingredients except the feta.

3. Cover with a tight-fitting lid and place in the oven and cook for 4-5 hours or until the lamb is soft and pulls apart easily with a fork. Remove from the heat, and shred lamb with a fork. Place lamb in a deep-sided pie dish (about 25cm round x 5cm deep) and add 5–7 tablespoons of the cooking liquid – you don't want the mixture to be runny, but you do want some liquid so that the meat doesn't dry out when you bake the pie. Crumble feta over lamb mixture.

4. **To make the topping,** gently pull apart the kataifi pastry to loosen the strands, and place in a bowl. Add the olive oil and, using your hands, gently toss the strands to coat them in the oil. Arrange the kataifi pastry evenly over the lamb and feta, pat down lightly, cover with foil and bake for 20 minutes, then remove the foil and cook for another 10 minutes or until the pastry is golden. Serve hot, sprinkled with a few basil leaves (if using).

Spicy braised lamb with apricots, pistachios and roast pumpkin

This is a great stew to serve on a cool day, perfect with steamed rice, a small pasta such as buttered orzo, or perhaps some steamed couscous. Chicken works well with these flavours too, just use thigh fillet and cook for a little less time than the lamb.

Gluten-free
🕐 **1–2 hours**
Serves 4

700g trimmed lamb shoulder
80ml extra virgin olive oil, plus extra
2 brown onions, cut into 1cm dice
1 tsp ground cinnamon
1 tsp ground cumin
4 cardamom pods, split, seeds
   removed and crushed
1 tsp of mild chilli flakes
2 tsp sea salt
2½ cups chicken stock
6 dried apricot halves, halved again
1 tsp caster sugar
juice of two limes
¼ tsp saffron threads, dissolved in
   1 tbsp boiling water
1 large handful of mint
2 tbsp chopped roasted pistachios,
   to serve

Roast pumpkin
400g butternut pumpkin, peeled
   and cut into 3½ cm pieces
1 tbsp extra virgin olive oil

1. To make the lamb stew, cut the lamb into 4cm pieces. Heat the oil in a heavy-based saucepan over high heat. Cook lamb, in batches, stirring, for about 5 minutes or until browned all over. Remove from the pan. Add extra oil to the pan if need be, turn heat to medium, add the onion and stir until lightly brown (about 8 minutes). Add the spices and sea salt and stir for one minute, or until fragrant. Add the stock.

2. Return lamb to the pan and simmer over a low heat, covered, or 1 hour, stirring occasionally. Add apricots, sugar, lime juice and saffron water. Cover and simmer for 30 minutes or until the lamb is very tender. Increase heat to medium-high and cook for 10–15 minutes until braising liquid is reduced and just coats the lamb.

3. Meanwhile, to make the pumpkin, preheat oven to 200°C (180°C fan-forced). Combine pumpkin with some sea salt and the oil. Put on a roasting tray lined with baking paper and bake for 20-30 minutes or until just tender and lightly browned all over.

4. Add the pumpkin and mint to the stew and stir through. Spoon into a large bowl and sprinkle with roasted pistachios to serve.

Chicken, duck and meat

Moroccan-style slow-roasted lamb leg with eggplant

Gluten-free
🕐 **2 hours +**
Serves 4

This dish is full of flavour, however, if you add something like an orange and fennel salad (or a date and orange salad), plus a bowl of couscous or rice, then you have the perfect meal. As for leftovers, the lamb is awesome for sandwiches and I like the eggplant served on toasted crusty bread with garlic rubbed on it and a drizzle of extra virgin olive oil. Alternatively, you can dice the lamb, fold it through the eggplant and spoon it on penne.

1 small lamb leg, bone-in
   (about 2kg)
olive oil and lemon wedges,
   to serve
couscous, rice or salad, to serve

Marinade
50g butter, softened
2 tbsp ground coriander
1 tbsp ground cumin
1 tbsp cumin seeds
1 tsp chilli flakes
4 garlic cloves, peeled and crushed
1 tsp crushed sea salt
freshly ground black pepper

Eggplant chermoula
2 medium eggplants, cut into
   2.5cm cubes, skin on
2 tsp sea salt
olive oil, for shallow-frying
2 cloves garlic, minced
1 tsp ground cumin
1 tsp sweet paprika
400g can chopped tomatoes
3 tbsp red wine vinegar
1 tsp clear honey

1. Preheat oven to 150°C (130°C fan-forced). Using a sharp paring knife, make deep incisions all over the lamb leg: this will help the flavours of the marinade get into the leg.

2. Place all marinade ingredients in a small bowl and mix thoroughly until a paste is formed. Use your hands to rub this paste all over the lamb leg, pushing it into the cuts in the leg as much as you can.

3. Place lamb on a wire rack in a roasting tray and roast for 4 hours, basting the lamb with its juices every 30 minutes or so. Cover with foil after 3 hours if the meat is browning too much.

4. Once cooked, remove lamb from the oven, cover with foil and rest for at least 30 minutes. Slice.

5. Meanwhile, make the eggplant chermoula. Season the eggplant with salt. Heat olive oil in a saucepan over medium heat (you'll need enough oil for about 1cm depth) and fry eggplant in batches until golden (about 5 minutes), turning regularly. Remove with a slotted spoon. Repeat until all eggplant is cooked. Drain any remaining oil into a heatproof bowl.

6. Return the pan to medium heat with 1 tbsp of fresh oil, add the garlic, cumin and paprika and stir, then add the tomatoes. Cook for a further 8-10 minutes, then add the vinegar and honey. Cook for a further 2 minutes or until reduced, then add the cooked eggplant. Stir through, remove the pan from the heat.

7. Place eggplant chermoula on serving plates and top with the sliced lamb. Drizzle with extra virgin olive oil, squeeze over some lemon juice and season. Serve with couscous, rice or a salad.

Chicken, duck and meat

goodfood

Beef rendang

⏱ **1–2 hours**
Serves 4

Curry favour with your guests by making them this mouthwatering beef rendang. It can be also made with lamb or chicken – just alter the cooking time. Using a small shoulder of lamb (about a kilogram) will take a little less time, while chicken thighs will be ready in 30 minutes.

3 tbsp vegetable oil
800g topside beef, cut into
   3cm pieces
600ml coconut milk
1½ tbsp tamarind paste
6 kaffir lime leaves, crushed,
   plus extra to serve
1½ tbsp grated palm sugar
sea salt
steamed jasmine rice and
   Asian greens, to serve

Rendang curry paste
15g shrimp paste
1 red onion, roughly chopped
8 garlic cloves, chopped
12 long red chillies, seeds removed
   and chopped
1 lemongrass stem, white part
   only, chopped
40g galangal, peeled and
   finely chopped
40g ginger, peeled and finely
   chopped
1 kaffir lime, finely grated zest
5g fresh turmeric, grated,
   or 1 tsp ground turmeric

1. Preheat oven to 160°C. To make the curry paste, first wrap the shrimp paste in foil and roast for about 10 minutes, until fragrant. Blend or process all the ingredients together to form a smooth paste (makes about 400g).

2. Heat the oil in a deep frying pan or wok. Add 150g curry paste and fry for 3 minutes – this will release a strong chilli fragrance, but it is a necessary part of the recipe and well worth it. (The remaining curry paste will keep for up to 3 months in a freezer.)

3. Add the beef, coconut milk, tamarind paste and kaffir lime leaves. Simmer, uncovered, stirring frequently (so the coconut milk doesn't stick) for 1-1½ hours, or until the meat is tender and the curry has thickened. Add palm sugar and salt to taste. Serve with extra finely sliced kaffir lime leaves, steamed jasmine rice and Asian greens.

Red-braised, caramelised pork belly with fresh finger limes

Gluten-free
🕐 **1–2 hours**
Serves 4

Red-braised master stock is the perfect stock for poaching and braising meat and poultry. Apart from pork belly, whole quails, pigeon, lamb ribs, duck breasts and beef brisket all work really well when red-braised. After cooking with the stock, you simply strain it and freeze it indefinitely to use again. It ages gracefully, developing a stronger flavour over time. You can, of course, substitute fresh lemon or lime cheeks for the finger limes.

3.5 litres red-braised master stock (see recipe below)
1 x 450g free-range boneless pork belly, skin on, at room temperature
1 cup brown sugar
1 cup water
2 tbsp fish sauce
juice of 1-2 lemons
½ tsp Sichuan peppercorns, crushed
4 fresh finger limes sliced in half lengthways (or use 2 x lemon or lime cheeks)

Master stock
4 spring onions, trimmed and halved
80g ginger, thickly sliced
6 cloves garlic, crushed
4 strips (about 6cm x 1cm) orange peel, white pith removed
8 whole star-anise
4 cinnamon quills
375ml light soy sauce*
250ml lightly packed dark brown sugar
1 tsp sesame oil
3 litres cold water

*Check soy sauce is gluten-free if required

1. **For the master stock**, place all ingredients in a large saucepan that will later hold the pork belly comfortably, and bring to the boil, stirring to dissolve sugar. Reduce heat to a gentle simmer and cook for 25 minutes to allow the flavours to infuse.

2. Meanwhile, place pork belly in a separate saucepan, cover with plenty of cold water and bring to the boil. Simmer for 10 minutes, then drain. This will remove any impurities from the meat.

3. After 25 minutes, return the stock to the boil. Lower pork belly into the stock, ensuring it is fully submerged – you may need to weigh it down with a plate – and poach pork gently for 3 hours or until the meat is very tender. There should be no more than an occasional ripple breaking the surface; adjust the temperature, if necessary. Do not put a lid on the pan at any stage. (Depending on the size of your pan, you may need to top up the stock with hot water during cooking to keep the pork submerged.) To check if it's ready, pierce the pork with a small knife – you should meet no resistance.

4. Remove pork from the pot and set aside on a plate lined with paper towel to drain thoroughly. When pork is cool enough to handle, carefully cut into large bite-sized pieces. After cooking with the stock, you can strain it and freeze it to use again. It will develop a stronger flavour over time.

5. Place brown sugar and water in a medium-sized pan and bring to the boil, then allow to caramelise, which will take about 6 minutes. Add the fish sauce and lemon juice.

6. Add pork pieces to hot caramel sauce and toss well. Place hot pork pieces in a serving dish, sprinkle with Sichuan pepper and salt flakes, and serve with freshly squeezed finger limes.

Chicken, duck and meat

Cider pork stew

🕐 **1–2 hours**
Serves 4–6

1 tbsp olive oil
600g pork belly, skin off, cut into
    4cm pieces
600g pork shoulder, skin off,
    cut into 4cm pieces
2 large brown onions, peeled
    and thickly sliced
2 tbsp brandy
5 sprigs thyme
1 tsp salt
375ml dry apple cider
2 tbsp seeded mustard
2 Granny Smith apples, peeled,
    cored and cut into wedges
100ml cream
boiled new potatoes, to serve

This autumnal dish makes great use of new-season
Granny Smith apples. A mix of belly and shoulder
pork gives the best texture.

1. Heat oil in a large, lidded casserole over a high heat and fry the
   pork belly pieces first until browned, then remove from the pot
   and fry the pork shoulder until browned. Remove the shoulder
   pieces from the pot and fry the onions in the same fat until
   lightly browned.

2. Return pork to the pot with the onion and add brandy, thyme,
   salt, apple cider and mustard. Stir well, cover and simmer for
   45 minutes. You may need to add a little water if the pot becomes
   too dry.

3. Add apples, cover again and continue simmering for a further
   15-20 minutes until the pork is tender but not falling apart.
   Stir through the cream, adjust for seasoning and serve with
   boiled new potatoes.

◆ **Tip** A side of boiled new potatoes is a classic that never goes out of style.
   Just scrub the potatoes until clean and cover with cold salted water.
   Simmer for 10-15 minutes, until tender, season with salt and dress with
   a little melted butter.

KATRINA MEYNINK

Soy and chilli pulled pork, coconut brown rice, pickled pineapple and greens

Healthy doesn't have to be boring. With Thai-inspired flavours, this grain bowl is as tasty as it is good for you.

🕐 **30 mins–1 hour**
Serves 4

Marinade
120g palm sugar, grated or crushed
125ml kecap manis
80ml fish sauce
2 tsp finely grated ginger
2 star anise, crushed
1 pork tenderloin or fillet
    (120g per serve)

Pickled pineapple
100ml apple cider vinegar
1½ tbsp caster sugar
juice of ½ lime
¼ pineapple, peeled, chopped into
    generous bite-sized pieces
½ tsp ground coriander

Herbed coconut rice
200g brown basmati rice
360ml coconut milk
150ml chicken stock
¼ cup Thai basil leaves,
    finely chopped
¼ cup Vietnamese mint leaves,
    finely chopped

Greens
1 bunch broccolini
olive oil for brushing
1 cup sugar snap peas, steamed

To serve
fresh coriander, mint, Thai basil,
    Vietnamese mint, coconut
    cream, fresh pieces of coconut

1. Combine marinade ingredients in a bowl. Add the pork tenderloin and set aside for 30 minutes.

2. Meanwhile, prepare the pickled pineapple by combining the vinegar, sugar, lime, coriander and 25ml water in a bowl; season to taste and stir until sugar dissolves. Add the pineapple pieces, stirring to coat, then cover and place in the fridge until ready to serve.

3. **To make the coconut rice,** bring coconut milk, rice and stock to the boil in a saucepan over medium heat. Cover with a tight-fitting lid, reduce heat to low and cook for 10–15 minutes. Keep checking on the rice, and if the liquid is evaporating too quickly, top up with water, about a tablespoon at a time. Once cooked, remove from heat, and stand until required. Once cooled, stir through the finely chopped herbs.

4. Heat a nonstick char-grill pan over medium heat, remove pork from marinade (reserving the marinade) and grill, turning occasionally, until charred and almost cooked through. Set the meat aside to rest.

5. Pour remaining marinade into a saucepan and place over medium heat and cook for 5 minutes until reduced. Using two forks or a knife and fork, pull apart the pork meat and add to the saucepan of reduced marinade, turning quickly and cooking until pork is glazed and sauce has thickened. Remove from heat.

6. For the broccolini, heat a grill or barbecue to high heat, brush broccolini with oil, and grill, turning occasionally, until charred and tender (4–5 minutes). Combine in a bowl with the steamed sugar snap peas.

7. To serve, place some pickled pineapple into each bowl. Add some herbed coconut rice and the steamed greens. Arrange the pork meat, then top with coconut cream, fresh coconut and any extra herbs. Serve immediately.

◆ **Note** If not serving immediately, assemble the bowl but do not add the coconut cream until ready to serve.

Slow-cooked Campari ribs

Gluten-free
🕐 **2 hours**
Serves 4–6

4 x 400g packs of barbecue
    pork ribs
4 tsp coarse sea salt

Spice rub
4 tsp ground cumin
4 tsp smoked sweet paprika
1-2 tsp chilli powder
½ tsp cinnamon
1 tsp cocoa

Campari glaze
2 tbsp Campari
2 tbsp brown sugar
2 tbsp tomato paste
salt to taste

A slow day at home means you can be around while these pork ribs cook to tenderness in the oven. When you're ready to eat they can be brushed with a bittersweet Campari glaze and quickly baked until sizzling. The Campari flavour is subtle, which is good, but if you want it more pronounced you could rub extra into the ribs before salting. Allow about five hours from salting to final baking with the glaze.

1. Place the ribs in a large bowl, rub the salt over them then place in the fridge for an hour. This salting helps to keep the ribs extra moist during their slow bake.

2. To make the spice rub, put the cumin, paprika, chilli powder, cinnamon and cocoa into a small bowl and mix well to combine.

3. Place the ribs in a roasting dish, pour in 200ml water to produce lots of steam, and sprinkle half the spices over. Rub spices into the ribs. Cover the dish tightly with foil, place in a cold oven, switch it on to 150°C (130°C fan-forced) and bake for about 3 hours.

4. Remove the dish from the oven, peel the foil back carefully, flip the ribs over and rub on the remaining spice, making sure there's still 1cm of water in the base of the dish.

5. Re-cover with foil and bake for a further hour, or until the meat is very tender. At this point you can cool, drain and refrigerate them.

6. To make the glaze, measure the Campari, sugar and tomato paste in a small bowl and stir to combine. Add salt to taste.

7. To serve, place the ribs on a baking tray covered with nonstick paper, brush with the Campari glaze, and bake at 190°C (170°C fan-forced) until piping hot and sizzling.

Chicken, duck and meat

Desserts and treats

Chocolate and coconut banana bread

Everybody loves banana bread, but I'm not sure it's a great choice for breakfast or brunch. Boosting it with chocolate takes it away from morning fare and puts it squarely in the realm of delicious desserts. Try it fried in butter and served with a scoop of ice-cream.

Easy
Nut-free
🕐 **1–2 hours**
Serves 8–10

4-5 large ripe bananas (about 2 cups after mashing)
½ cup melted butter, plus extra for greasing
¾ cup soft brown sugar
1 tsp salt
2 eggs, beaten
1 tsp vanilla extract
¼ cup cocoa powder
2 cups plain flour
2 tsp baking powder
½ tsp baking soda
½ cup fine desiccated coconut
½ cup grated couverture chocolate

1. Preheat oven to 175°C. In a large bowl, mash the bananas with a fork. Add butter, sugar, salt, eggs and vanilla and mix well. In a separate bowl combine the cocoa powder, flour, baking powder and baking soda and mix well. Gently mix the flour mixture with the wet ingredients until well combined, then fold through the coconut and chocolate.

2. Transfer to a greased 23cm x 13cm loaf pan and bake for 1 hour. Test with a skewer and, if needed, bake for up to another 15 minutes. Allow to cool slightly in the tin, then turn out and slice to serve.

◆ **Tip** Couverture chocolate contains a higher percentage of cocoa butter than chocolate chips, which means it will be shinier and make your banana cake more moist, but you can use chocolate chips if you wish.

Desserts and treats

ADAM LIAW

Caramelised pineapple and fennel upside-down cake

This ingredient combination may seem strange, but the aniseed flavour of fennel combines with the tartness of pineapple to make a fantastic match.

Nut-free
🕐 **30 mins–1 hour**
Serves 8–10

¼ cup white sugar
1 small fennel bulb, cut into thin half-moons (reserve fronds for garnish)
25g butter, plus extra for greasing
½ small pineapple, peeled, cored and thinly sliced lengthways into wedges
2 tbsp brown sugar
300ml double cream, to serve

Cake batter
2 cups plain flour
1 tsp baking powder
1 tsp ground fennel
½ tsp salt
150g butter
½ cup sugar
2 eggs
1 tsp vanilla extract

1. Combine white sugar and 1½ cups water in a small pan, bring to a simmer, add the fennel and cook for 10 minutes, until tender. Drain, reserving 2 tablespoons of the fennel water.

2. In a frying pan, heat the butter, add the pineapple and cook for about 3 minutes until lightly browned. Add the brown sugar and stir gently to create a caramel. Stir in the drained fennel and reserved fennel water, ensuring that the caramel thoroughly coats the pineapple and fennel. Arrange the pineapple and fennel in the base of a greased and lined 22cm-diameter cake tin.

3. Preheat oven to 180°C. For the cake batter, place the flour, baking powder, ground fennel and salt in a bowl and mix to combine. In a separate bowl, or the basin of a stand mixer, cream the butter and sugar together until pale and fluffy. Beat in the eggs, 1 at a time, then mix through the vanilla. Add the dry ingredients a little at a time, mixing at a slow speed to form a smooth batter.

4. Pour the batter over the pineapple and fennel and bake for 35 minutes or until the top of the cake is golden brown and a skewer inserted into the centre comes out clean. Allow to cool in the tin, then turn out onto a serving platter. Garnish with the reserved fennel fronds and serve with cream.

Banana, coffee and cardamom bundt cake with coffee caramel

Nut-free
🕐 **1 hour 10 mins**
Serves 8–10

130g unsalted butter, cut into 2cm
    cubes, at room temperature, plus
    extra for greasing
150g golden caster sugar
2 eggs, at room temperature
1 tsp vanilla extract
220g self-raising flour, plus extra
    for dusting
¼ tsp salt
1 tsp ground cardamom
2–3 overripe medium bananas,
    peeled and mashed (about 250g)
100g sour cream
¼ tsp bicarbonate of soda
30ml strong black coffee, chilled
whipped cream, to serve

Coffee caramel
120g caster sugar
85ml double cream
30ml strong black coffee

I love a banoffee pie, but often find it cloying after the first few mouthfuls. Here I have taken the banana, coffee and caramel (toffee) of the traditional pie, added cardamom to complement them, and turned it into a cake.

1. Preheat oven to 180°C (160°C fan-forced). Brush the inside of a bundt tin with some softened butter, then dust with flour and tap away excess. Place in the freezer while you prepare the rest of the cake.

2. Combine butter and sugar in an electric mixer fitted with the paddle attachment, and beat on medium-high speed for about 3 minutes, until light but not too fluffy. Add eggs, 1 at a time, beating well after each addition, then add vanilla extract and mix until combined. The batter may look a little curdled at this point – don't worry, it will come together with the remaining ingredients.

3. Sift flour, salt and cardamom in a medium bowl and set aside.

4. Place mashed banana in another medium bowl, add sour cream, bicarb soda and coffee. Alternately add the banana mix and flour mix to the butter and sugar, beating on low speed. When combined, spoon the mixture into the prepared tin. It should come three-quarters of the way up the sides.

5. Bake for 40–45 minutes or until a skewer inserted into the centre of the cake comes out clean. Remove from the oven and allow to cool for 10 minutes before turning out onto a serving plate.

6. While the cake is baking, make the coffee caramel. Place sugar and 100ml cold water in a medium pan and stir to combine. Bring to a boil, then simmer over medium-high heat without stirring. Instead, swirl the pan gently from time to time, and when the caramel turns a deep amber colour (8–10 minutes), reduce heat and carefully add the cream and coffee. Stir until smooth, then remove from heat and allow to cool and thicken slightly before drizzling over the cake. Serve with whipped cream.

Lemon and raspberry loaf cake

Easy
Nut-free
🕐 **1 hour 10 mins**
Serves 8–10

3 large eggs
225g caster sugar
120ml double cream
75g unsalted butter, cubed finely
grated zest of 3 lemons (1 tbsp)
170g plain flour
1¼ tsp baking powder
¼ tsp salt
150g fresh raspberries

Glaze
100g icing sugar
2 tbsp lemon juice

It seems to amuse people that this simple bake is the one
I would take to my desert island. It has a very pleasant
texture, sort of a cross between a layer cake and a Genoise
sponge. Without the acidity and sweet syrup of a lemon
drizzle cake, it's an altogether gentler offering, with the
fragrance of lemons coming mostly from the zest. You could
add a tablespoon or two of poppyseeds for a pop of texture,
but raspberries work beautifully for this summer variation.

1. Preheat oven to 175°C. Line a 20cm x 12cm loaf tin with baking
   paper and set aside.

2. Place the eggs and sugar in the bowl of an electric mixer fitted with
   the whisk attachment and beat on a medium-high speed for about
   2 minutes until pale and frothy. Add cream and continue to whisk
   at same speed for about 2 minutes, until mixture is well combined
   and slightly thickened.

3. Meanwhile, melt butter in a small saucepan over a low heat,
   add lemon zest and set aside to cool to room temperature.

4. Sift flour, baking powder and salt together into a small bowl, then
   use a spatula to fold this into the egg mixture. Add raspberries,
   then gently fold through the melted butter and zest.

5. Spoon the mixture into prepared tin so it reaches three-quarters
   of the way up the sides. Place the tin on a baking tray and bake for
   about 55 minutes or until a skewer inserted into the centre comes
   out clean. Resist the temptation to open the door for the first
   45 minutes.

6. Make the glaze by whisking the icing sugar with the lemon juice
   in a bowl. Allow the cake to cool for 15 minutes before removing
   from tin and onto a serving platter, then spoon over the glaze.
   The cake will keep for about three days, wrapped in plastic wrap

◆ **Tip** For a slightly crusty glaze and more lemony cake, pour over glaze as
   soon as the cake comes out of the oven while still in the tin and let it cool
   for about 30 minutes.

Desserts and treats

goodfood

Molasses and coconut rum cake with vanilla and coconut icing

Nut-free
🕐 **1–2 hours**
Serves 4–6

100g molasses or black treacle
100g dark brown sugar
2 tsp ground ginger
2 tsp ground cinnamon
100g unsalted butter
50g coconut milk
2 eggs (about 60g each)
2 tsp vanilla extract
100g desiccated coconut
150g strong bread flour
2 tsp baking powder
dark rum to finish

Vanilla bean and coconut icing (optional)
150g icing sugar
1-2 tbsp coconut milk
½ tsp vanilla bean paste
sweetened coconut flakes,
   to decorate

A generous glug of dark rum turns the texture of this dark coconut cake extra moist and sticky, perfect to eat on its own without icing. But if you want to glam it up, ultra-white vanilla icing will make it dazzle on your table for friends.

1. Line base and sides of a medium loaf tin with non-stick baking paper and heat the oven to 180°C (160°C fan-forced).

2. Put the molasses in a saucepan with the sugar, ginger and cinnamon and warm until any lumps in the sugar soften and the mixture is smooth, but not boiling. Pour this into a mixing bowl, add the butter and stir until it melts.

3. Beat in the coconut milk followed by the eggs and vanilla, then stir in the coconut. Sift together the flour and baking powder then stir these through.

4. Spoon the mixture into prepared tin and bake for about 50 minutes or until firm in the middle. Remove from the oven and leave to cool then generously slosh some rum over the top and leave it to soak in.

5. While the cake cools, put the icing sugar in a small bowl and stir in enough coconut milk, a little at a time, to make a smooth, thick icing. Beat in the vanilla paste. When the cake is cold, spread on the icing, sprinkle with coconut flakes and leave to set before slicing to serve.

Coconut pearl cake

Vegan
Gluten-free
Nut-free
🕐 **1 hour**
Serves 4–6

1 cup cold water
10g cornflour or gluten-free
    flour mix
20g fine tapioca pearls
3 tsp ground chia seeds
1 tsp ground turmeric
1 tsp ground allspice
100g coconut milk
1 tsp vinegar
20g desiccated coconut
180g white gluten-free flour mix
½ tsp bicarbonate of soda
½ tsp baking powder
80g raw, coconut or muscovado
    sugar
flaked coconut and extra sugar,
    to serve

Delicately sweet and rich with coconut, this vegan and
gluten-free cake has a simple but elegant bake-on topping,
which means that once it's in the oven you can clean up and
relax. I call it a "pearl cake" because of the tapioca pearls in
the crumb, barely noticeable but the key reason it keeps so
well. It stays soft for days, so you can make it ahead and store
it in the cake tin.

1. Line base of a round 18cm round cake tin and preheat oven to
   180°C (160°C fan-forced).

2. Place water in a saucepan, whisk in the cornflour, add the tapioca
   and bring to the boil, stirring constantly. Remove from the heat
   and scrape into a large mixing bowl. Whisk in the ground chia,
   turmeric and allspice, followed by the coconut milk and the vinegar.

3. In a small bowl mix together the desiccated coconut, white flour
   mix, bicarbonate of soda, baking powder and sugar. Stir the dry
   ingredients together evenly, breaking up any sugar lumps, then stir
   them through the tapioca mixture until just combined but no more
   (as the bicarb will have started to bubble).

4. Scrape the batter into the tin, then smooth the top with a very
   wet pastry brush. Sprinkle the top with sugar, then flaked coconut,
   and bake for about 40 minutes, until the cake feels firm and pulls
   away slightly form the side of the tin. The coconut turns a deep
   golden brown, so if you want it lighter, cover the top of the cake
   with foil for the last 15 minutes of baking. Leave to cool in the
   tin, then serve.

Cumquat and almond upside-down cake

1–2 hours
Serves 10

Cumquats make the best marmalade, so I recently set a box of the fruit aside to make jam. However, an unseasonably warm weekend made me a bit impatient, and halfway through the slicing and pipping of the little orange orbs, I decided to turn them into a cake – a very happy outcome. A word of caution: don't use a cake tin with a removable base, as the sugar and cumquats form a caramel that will seep out onto the floor of your oven.

For the cumquats
500g cumquats
160g raw caster sugar

For the batter
250g unsalted butter, at room
  temperature
250g golden caster sugar
4 large eggs (at room temperature),
  lightly beaten
2 tsp brandy
120g self-raising flour
¼ tsp salt
140g almond meal
thickened cream, to serve

1. Preheat oven to 190°C (180°C fan-forced), and line the base and sides of a 23cm round cake tin with baking paper.

2. Remove any stalks from the cumquats, then cut in half (or thirds if they are large), de-seeding as you go. Place the sliced cumquats in a bowl, add the raw caster sugar and toss gently. Set aside while you prepare the cake batter.

3. Place the butter and golden caster sugar in the bowl of an electric mixer, fitted with the paddle attachment and beat on medium speed until lightened. Add the beaten egg, a little at a time, scraping down the sides of the bowl every now and again. The mixture may curdle a little, but don't worry, it will come together again. Add the brandy and beat until combined.

4. Sift flour and salt into a bowl, then stir in the almond meal. With the speed of the mixer on medium-low, add the dry ingredients in three batches.

5. Tip the macerating sugared cumquats into the prepared tin (including any juice and syrup) and use a spatula to spread the cumquats so that they are evenly distributed over the base of the tin. Scrape the cake batter gently over the top of the cumquats, smoothing over so that it is even.

6. Place in the oven and bake for 50–55 minutes or until a skewer inserted into the centre comes out clean. Remove from the oven and set aside to cool for 15 minutes before turning out onto a cake platter – be careful, as there may be some hot cumquat syrup in the tin. Serve warm or at room temperature with thickened cream.

Desserts and treats

Double chocolate olive oil cake with white chocolate mascarpone buttercream

30 mins – 1 hour
Serves 8–10

The combination of cocoa plus melted dark chocolate gives this cake very rich flavour and texture and it keeps soft for days. The olive oil flavour is clear but subtle, but you can replace it with any vegetable oil for a more regular flavour. Ditto the coffee; for children you might want to try using warm milk or fruit juice instead. Need a simple finish? Sweetened whipped cream in place of the buttercream works a treat.

300g dark muscovado or
    brown sugar
350ml milk (for dairy-free, see tips
    in method)
2 eggs (60g each)
100ml extra virgin olive oil
100g dark (70 per cent)
    chocolate, melted
250g plain flour
75g cocoa powder
1 tsp baking powder
½ tsp bicarbonate of soda
100ml hot black regular coffee,
    not espresso-strength

**White chocolate mascarpone
buttercream**
250g unsalted butter, soft at room
    temperature
250g icing sugar
150g mascarpone
200g white chocolate, melted

1. Line bases of two deep round 20cm sponge tins (not the removable base kind as the cake batter is quite liquid) with non-stick paper, and preheat oven to 180°C (160°C fan forced).

2. Put the sugar in a bowl and whisk in the milk. Whisk in the eggs then the oil and melted chocolate.

3. Sift in the flour, cocoa, baking powder and bicarbonate, whisk until smooth then beat in the coffee. The mixture will be a very liquid, thick soup consistency, but don't worry. Pour it evenly into the tins and bake for about 45 minutes or until a skewer poked in the centre comes out clean.

4. Meanwhile, make the buttercream. Beat the butter with the icing sugar until smooth. Add the mascarpone and beat until just combined, no more. Then add the melted white chocolate and beat again until just combined and fluffy.

5. Spread half of this over the top of one cake, sit the other cake on it, then finish with the remaining icing (you will have some left over). The buttercream will store well, covered in the fridge – just bring to room temperature and gently beat again until smooth to use.

Tips

◆ The cake can be made dairy-free easily, by replacing the milk with almond milk or juice, and decorating with a simple chocolate icing.

◆ The buttercream is utterly extravagant, and perfect for a bittersweet chocolate cake. The trick to keeping the texture light is to avoid overbeating it. Makes more than you need to cover and sandwich a 20cm round cake thickly.

Pumpkin bulgur wheat cake with saffron mahleb icing

① 1–2 hours
Serves 8–10

The combination of pumpkin and bulgur wheat is a classic; there's a gourd and grain harmony that kicks in. In this simple honey butter cake loaded with grated pumpkin, the bulgur adds a curious chewiness reminiscent of ground almonds. If you want to go nut-free, just leave out the walnuts and extract, but you'll need to whack a little texture back in so replace it with chopped dried apricots or figs. The icing is a must, especially if you can find the ground mahleb.

50g bulgur wheat
80g melted butter
80g dark honey, such as red gum
80g caster sugar
2 eggs (60g each)
finely grated zest of 1 lemon
20g lemon juice
100g peeled pumpkin,
   coarsely grated
125g chopped walnuts
200g plain flour
¾ tsp bicarbonate of soda
½ tsp ground cardamom

Icing
30g boiling water
pinch of saffron, optional
225g icing sugar
¾ tsp ground mahleb (spice made
   from cherry seeds), or 1 drop
   almond extract

1. Place bulgur wheat in a large saucepan. Pour on twice its volume in water, bring to the boil then put the lid on and leave off the heat to cool. The bulgur should absorb all the water and have a slightly chewy texture.

2. Line the base of a round, 18cm springform cake tin with non-stick paper and preheat oven to 160°C fan-forced. Place the cooked bulgur wheat in a mixing bowl and add the melted butter, honey, sugar and eggs, then whisk together well.

3. Stir in the lemon zest and juice, grated pumpkin and walnuts. Combine the flour, bicarbonate of soda and cardamom, then sift in and mix evenly. Spoon into prepared tin and bake for 40–50 minutes or until a skewer inserted into the centre comes out clean. Leave to cool in the tin before turning out.

4. To make the icing, weigh the water straight into a small bowl (easier than using a measuring spoon). Stir in the saffron, if using, and leave for 10 minutes. Stir in the icing sugar and mahleb (or almond extract) until smooth and spread over the cake.

Desserts and treats

goodfood

Cinnamon crumb pound cake

🕐 **30 mins–1 hour**
Serves 8–10

This classic's name hails from its ingredients – a pound each of butter, sugar and flour. This one gets a delicious crumb makeover.

455g unsalted butter, at room
    temperature
2 cups caster sugar
finely grated rind of 1 orange
2 tsp vanilla extract
8 eggs
¼ tsp salt
3 cups plain flour
3 tsp ground cinnamon
¾ cup pure icing sugar, sifted
1 tbsp milk, plus extra if needed

Cinnamon crumb mix
45g butter, melted
2 tbsp brown sugar
1 tbsp raw sugar
1 tsp vanilla extract
1 tsp ground cinnamon
¼ tsp salt
⅔ cup plain flour

1. To make the cinnamon crumb mix, combine all of the ingredients in a bowl. Set aside.

2. Preheat oven to 170°C. Grease and line a 24cm round cake tin.

3. Using an electric mixer, beat the butter, sugars, orange rind and 1 tsp of the vanilla extract together until thick and pale. With the mixer on medium speed, beat in the eggs, 1 at a time, until combined, scraping down the sides of the bowl as you go. Turn the mixer to low speed and add the salt, then the flour in thirds, mixing until just combined.

4. Pour half the cake batter into the cake pan. Sprinkle with half the ground cinnamon, then one-third of the crumb mix. Pour over remaining batter. Sprinkle with remaining ground cinnamon and crumb mixture. Bake for about 80 minutes or until a skewer inserted into the centre comes out clean. Remove from oven and allow to cool completely.

5. Whisk the icing sugar, milk and remaining vanilla extract in a bowl and drizzle over the cooled cake.

Pineapple jam and lime tarts

**⏲ 2 hours +
Makes 12**

I hope my Malaysian aunties will forgive me for giving this traditional Chinese New Year pastry a bit of a makeover with a lighter crust and a zest of lime rather than the usual cloves.

Pineapple jam
1 large pineapple (about 1.5kg), peeled, cored and chopped into 4-5cm pieces (you should have around 700g)
150g caster sugar
zest and juice of 1 lime

Pastry
300g plain flour
90g icing sugar, plus extra, for dusting
¼ tsp salt
200g unsalted butter, cold, cut into cubes, plus an extra 10g, melted, for brushing tins
grated zest of 1 lime (1 tsp)
1 large egg yolk, plus 1 large egg for glazing
20ml ice-cold water

1. To make the jam, pulse pineapple in a food processor to form a coarse puree. Strain through a fine sieve into a bowl, but do not press down on the puree; the aim is simply to remove excess juice.

2. Combine puree, sugar, zest and juice in a medium saucepan over medium-low heat and stir until the sugar has dissolved. Increase heat to medium, bring to a boil, then simmer for about an hour, stirring every 5–10 minutes with a wooden spoon. You may need to lower the heat a bit, and stir more frequently as the mixture thickens, to prevent it catching on the bottom of the pan. It will be ready when it is a thick golden paste (thicker than regular jam) and holds its shape when spooned on to a plate. Remove from heat and transfer to a bowl to cool. Store in the fridge (for up to two weeks) until ready to assemble the tarts.

3. For the pastry, sift together the flour, icing sugar and salt and place in a food processor. Add the butter and zest, then pulse a few times until the mixture is the consistency of breadcrumbs. Lightly whisk the egg yolk and water, and add to mix, pulsing just to combine.

4. Tip the dough out onto a lightly floured surface – it will be quite wet and sticky. Dust your hands lightly with flour, and press or pat gently to form a ball, then divide the pastry into two. Wrap each half loosely in plastic wrap and press gently to form two flattish discs. The dough will be soft and must be chilled for at least an hour (and up to 3 days) before using. (You will only be using one disc for these tarts. Freeze the other for another time.)

5. Brush moulds of a 12-hole patty pan lightly with melted butter.

6. Place 1 of the pastry discs on a lightly floured surface. Tap all over with a lightly floured rolling pin to soften slightly before rolling out to 2mm thick. Using a 7cm cookie cutter, stamp out 12 circles and place one in each greased mould. Gather offcuts and press together, then wrap in plastic wrap and return to the fridge (they will be rolled out to form lids for the tarts later).

7. Preheat oven to 180°C. Spoon a heaped tablespoon of the pineapple jam into each pastry case (note: the cases are not blind-baked). Level the surface with the back of a teaspoon.

8. Set the tray aside in a cool place while you roll out the pastry for the "lids": roll out the offcut pastry ball of dough to about 2mm thickness. Stamp out circles (or other shapes) or cut into strips to form a lattice design. Place the pastry circles or strips to form

goodfood

a "lid" or lattice on top of each tart. Brush the beaten egg over the
pastry top (avoiding contact with the pineapple jam).

9. Bake for about 25 minutes or until the pastry is golden brown all over.
   Allow to cool on the tray for 10 minutes before transferring to a wire
   rack to cool completely. Use a sieve to dust tarts with extra icing sugar.

♦ These tarts will keep, loosely wrapped in foil, for 3 to 4 days, though the jammy
  filling means they will get a bit softer over time.

goodfood

Date and walnut eccles cakes

2 hours +
Makes 12

I have taken the idea of a Lancashire Eccles cake and drawn on a Middle Eastern date-filled ma'amoul biscuit to create this delicious pastry. Retaining the hockey puck shape of the traditional Eccles cake, a northern English treat, I've used a "rough puff" as a shell for the date and walnut filling which is lightly scented with orange blossom water. The secret is in the contrast between the sticky, slightly caramelised date mixture and the light, flaky pastry.

Pastry
250g strong white bread flour
1 tsp fine sea salt
250g butter, cold, cut into
  2-3cm cubes
125ml ice-cold water
1 tsp lemon juice

Filling
2 tsp orange zest (from
  1 medium orange)
60ml orange juice
50g coconut oil (or unsalted butter)
50g dark brown sugar
¼ tsp salt
200g pitted dates (chopped into
  roughly 1cm pieces)
2 tsp ground cinnamon
1 tsp orange blossom water
40g walnuts, roughly chopped

Pastry topping
20g walnuts, finely chopped
20g sugar
1 eggwhite, lightly beaten

1. Sift flour and salt into a large bowl, then rub in the butter loosely with your fingertips. You want large flakes so be careful not to overmix. Combine water and lemon juice and sprinkle over the dough, mixing lightly to form a shaggy mixture, with bits of butter visible. Gather the pastry together, then shape roughly into a rectangular block and wrap loosely in plastic wrap. Chill for 30 minutes.

2. Roll out the pastry on a lightly floured surface to a 40cm x 20cm rectangle. The dough will still look quite rough at this stage, with streaks of butter. Fold the top third of the pastry (short end) down to the middle, then fold the bottom third up, so that they overlap. Turn the dough so that the seam is now on the right, and roll into a 40cm x 20cm rectangle, folding into thirds as before. Wrap in plastic wrap and place in the fridge for 30 minutes to rest.

3. **To make the filling,** combine orange zest and juice, coconut oil, sugar and salt in a medium saucepan and stir gently over low heat. When the coconut oil has melted, increase heat and simmer for 1 minute until syrupy. Remove from heat and add dates, cinnamon, orange blossom water and walnut. Stir to combine, then set aside to cool completely to a soft paste. Divide into 12 balls and place on a large plate. (The mixture may be refrigerated for up to three days.)

4. Preheat oven to 205°C. Cut pastry in half. One at a time, roll out to a thickness of about 4mm, then use a side plate (or saucepan lid) of about 12cm diameter to trace and cut out circles of pastry. Refrigerate them while you repeat with the other block of pastry. Re-roll the pastry offcuts if necessary, to make 12 circles.

5. Place a date ball into the centre of each pastry circle, gather up the sides and pinch to seal in the middle. Place on parchment-lined baking trays, seam-side down, spaced 3cm–4cm apart, then flatten gently. Repeat with remaining pastry and date mix.

6. Combine walnut and sugar in a bowl. Brush the tops of the pastries with eggwhite then sprinkle with walnut sugar mixture. Use the tip of a small knife to make two small cuts in the middle of each pastry. Bake for about 30 minutes, or until lightly browned. Serve.

Date and frangipane tart

① 1–2 hours
Serves 8–10

Any dried or cooked fruit will work beautifully in this frangipane tart.

250ml apple juice
125ml brandy
12 halved fresh dates, pitted
150g plum jam
icing sugar, to dust
300ml thickened cream, whipped,
   to serve

Pastry
250g plain flour
70g unsalted butter, softened
pinch of sea salt
90g icing sugar, sifted
60ml milk
2 egg yolks

Frangipane filling
125g unsalted butter, softened
125g icing sugar, sifted
3 eggs
125g almond meal
25g plain flour

1. To make the pastry, place the flour, butter, sea salt and icing sugar in a food processor and process for 20 seconds until fine breadcrumb consistency. Add the milk and egg yolks and process for 20-30 seconds into a dough.

2. Turn out the dough onto a lightly floured surface and knead gently for a few moments. Form into a ball, place in plastic wrap and refrigerate for 1 hour.

3. Lightly butter and flour a 24cm-diameter x 2.5cm round flan tin. Roll out pastry on a floured bench until about 3mm thick. Cut out a circle 5cm wider than tart case. Gently ease pastry into case, pushing the sides in gently. Allow to rest in fridge for 30 minutes.

4. Preheat oven to 180°C. Cut off any excess pastry and prick the base a few times with a fork. Line tart case with baking paper, add uncooked rice and bake for 20-25 minutes. Remove rice and baking paper and return pastry case to oven and bake for 5-10 minutes, until base has dried out.

5. Combine apple juice and brandy in a saucepan, bring to the boil, then add dates and simmer, uncovered, for 2 minutes. Drain dates and set aside. Drain and reserve the liquid, setting aside 25ml for frangipane, then reduce remaining liquid in pan over medium high heat until syrupy, about 6 minutes. Set aside to cool.

6. To make frangipane filling, use an electric mixer to beat butter in a large bowl until light and creamy. Add sugar and mix until well combined. Add the eggs, 1 at a time, mixing well after each addition. Gently stir in the almond meal, flour and 25ml reserved apple-brandy mixture and mix well. Cover and refrigerate for 30 minutes.

7. Preheat oven to 180°C. Spread the plum jam over the base of the tart shell, top with the drained dates and gently spoon enough of the filling over the jam and dates to cover. Bake for 35–40 minutes. Cool until just warm, dust with icing sugar.

8. Serve the tart with the whipped cream, drizzled with reduced apple-brandy mixture.

ANDREW
McCONNELL

Caramelised pear clafoutis

○ **30 mins–1 hour**
Serves 4

The simplicity of clafoutis is not its only appeal. This batter-style cake is the perfect vehicle for fruits that happen to be in season throughout the year. Although traditionally baked with cherries, other fruits work just as well. When cherries are in season, try replacing the pear in this recipe with a good amount of whole pitted cherries. Other fruit l like to use are apricots or figs. All of these cook well and complement the flavour of the almonds in the clafoutis.

goodfood

½ cup (125ml) cream
½ cup (125ml) milk
80g sugar
3 eggs
½ vanilla bean, split and
    seeds removed
pinch of salt
200g ground almonds
1 tsp either Kirsch, Grand
    Marnier or Cointreau
zest of ½ a lemon
1 tbsp flour
1 tbsp melted butter
caramelised pears (see
    recipe, below)
1 tbsp sugar, extra

Chantilly cream
150 ml whipping cream
100 ml creme fraiche
3 tbsp caster sugar

4 firm packham pears
1 vanilla bean
2 tbsp soft butter
4 tbsp sugar
100ml water
1 tsp Poire William* or brandy
    (optional)

1. In a blender or stand mixer fitted with the whisk attachment, blend the cream, milk, sugar, eggs, vanilla seeds and salt for 1 minute. Add the ground almonds, liqueur, lemon zest and flour followed by the melted butter, and blend for 1 another minute or until smooth. Leave the batter to rest for half an hour before using.

2. Preheat oven to 180°C.

3. Pour the batter into a buttered frying pan (about 14cm), ceramic or enamel baking dish. Strategically place the caramelised pears into the clafoutis, ensuring the wedges are evenly spaced and not touching each other.

4. Bake for 15 minutes – when the clafoutis has begun to set, remove from the oven, sprinkle the top with 1 tablespoon of sugar and return to the oven for another 10-15 minutes or until set. The clafoutis is ready when firm to touch and light brown. To test, pierce the centre with a small knife; it should come out clean when cooked.

5. To make the chantilly cream, in a bowl or blender with the whisk attachment, vigorously whisk the cream, creme fraiche and sugar together. Continue to whisk until the cream has started to thicken to soft peaks. Store the whipped cream in the fridge until ready to serve.

6. Let the clafoutis cool to room temperature before serving at the table with chantilly cream.

Caramelised pears for clafoutis

1. Peel, quarter and core the pears. Heat an enamel or stainless steel frying pan that will house the pears tightly. The pears should form a snug single layer in the base of the pan and not be stacked up on top of each other.

2. Split the vanilla bean and scrape out the seeds with the back of a knife. Julienne (finely shred) the remaining vanilla pod and set aside.

3. Add the butter, sugar and prepared pears to the pan. Place the pan over a high heat and gently saute, moving the pears about from time to time as they caramelise. When they are caramelised, add the water, brandy and vanilla bean.

4. Cover with a tight-fitting lid or aluminium foil, turn down the heat to a low and cook for 10 minutes, checking occasionally and adding more water as it evaporates. Once cooked remove the lid and simmer stirring occasionally until all the liquid has completely reduced. Set the pears aside to cool until ready to add to the clafoutis.

Flourless chocolate and orange puddings

Gluten-free
🕐 **30 mins–1 hour**
Serves 6–8

30g caster sugar
1 tsp ground anise seeds
30g unsalted butter, softened

Batter
300g cooking chocolate (about
   60 per cent cocoa solids),
   roughly chopped
1 tbsp finely grated orange zest
4 large eggs, at room temperature
60g caster sugar
120ml double cream
200g creme fraiche, to serve

You don't want to use a chocolate that is too dark or bitter in this recipe, because there is not a lot of sugar. If serving as a hot pudding, use small ovenproof ramekins or moulds you can take straight to the table. If making ahead, allow the puddings to sit for 10 minutes before inverting onto serving plates.

1. Preheat oven to 190°C (170°C fan-forced). Combine the 30g of sugar with the anise in a small bowl and set aside. Brush the ramekins or moulds generously with the softened butter, then sprinkle the anise sugar to coat evenly, tapping away any excess. Place the prepared ramekins in a large, deep baking dish and set aside.

2. Place chocolate in a medium heatproof bowl set over a pan of simmering water, making sure the base of the bowl isn't touching the water. Stir gently with a spatula from time to time to ensure the chocolate melts evenly. Once melted, remove the bowl from the heat, stir in the orange zest and set aside to cool for 10 minutes.

3. Place eggs and sugar in the bowl of an electric mixer fitted with the whisk attachment and beat on high for about 6 minutes, until the mixture is light and fluffy, and has tripled in volume. Meanwhile, place the cream in a medium bowl and whisk by hand or with a hand-held electric whisk until very soft peaks form.

4. Remove the bowl (with eggs and sugar) from the mixer. Gently fold in the chocolate, in 2 batches, using a rubber spatula. When almost combined – there will be some streaks – fold in whipped cream until combined. It will lose a little volume, but be careful not to overmix.

5. Spoon mixture into prepared ramekins, filling them three-quarters of the way up the sides. Transfer the baking dish to the oven and carefully pour just-boiled water into the tray, so that it rises a third of the way up the sides. Bake for 20–22 minutes or until the puddings are softly set in the middle; check by gently tapping the centre with your fingers. Carefully remove the baking dish from the oven and, using oven gloves, transfer the ramekins on to serving plates. Alternatively, allow the puddings to rest for 10 minutes before inverting onto serving plates. Serve with creme fraiche.

Desserts and treats

Lemon raspberry meringue pie

🕐 **1–2 hours**
Serves 6–8

1 portion basic sweet pastry
(recipe on page 204)
fresh basil leaves, to serve
(optional)

Lemon curd filling
3 eggs, plus 1 egg yolk
160g caster sugar
150ml fresh lemon juice (from
about 4 lemons)
zest of 3 lemons
100g butter
1 gold strength gelatin sheet,
softened in ice-cold water

Cardamom raspberry layer
150g fresh raspberries
1 tsp vanilla bean paste
1 tsp ground cardamom

Italian meringue
330g caster sugar
5 eggwhites

It's important to add the gelatine to the lemon curd to ensure it holds the layer of raspberry and the glorious top hat of meringue. A few fresh basil leaves are the perfect partner to this sweet-but-tart showstopping pie. Note: You will need a candy thermometer for the meringue.

1. Preheat oven to 200°C. Grease and line a pie tin. Gently place the rolled and chilled pastry over the top and push into the tin, trimming the sides. Chill for 20 minutes.

2. Line tin with baking paper and fill with pastry weights or uncooked rice, then blind bake the pastry for 20–25 minutes or until golden around the edges. Remove weights or rice and return to the oven for a further 10 minutes – the case should take on a lovely tanned appearance. Remove from the oven and allow to cool.

3. **For the lemon curd,** whisk eggs, yolk and sugar in a heatproof bowl, then whisk in lemon juice and zest, followed by the butter. Place the bowl over a saucepan of simmering water (do not allow the water to boil) and lightly whisk for about 20 minutes until it thickens to the consistency of whipped cream. Remove from the heat, and working quickly, add the bloomed gelatine and whisk briskly to combine and prevent any clumps from forming.

4. Spoon the curd into the cooked, cooled pastry shell and smooth the top using the back of the spoon. Place in the fridge for 30 minutes or until completely cooled and just set – it should be wobbly, and slightly softer than a panna cotta in consistency.

5. **For the cardamom raspberry layer,** using a fork, mash the raspberries with the vanilla and cardamom in a bowl until the juices are released. Gently spread the mixture over the lemon curd then return to the fridge while you prepare the meringue.

6. **For the Italian meringue,** place sugar in a heavy-based saucepan, add ¼ cup water and stir over low heat until sugar dissolves. Increase heat to high and cook until syrup reaches 115°C on a sugar thermometer, then remove from heat. Meanwhile, using an electric mixer, whisk eggwhites until soft peaks form, then, with the motor running, slowly pour in the hot sugar syrup in a steady stream and whisk for 5 minutes or until the bowl no longer feels warm to the touch. Reduce speed to low and mix until the meringue reaches room temperature.

7. Scoop the meringue mixture onto the pie, and gently use your spoon to create peaks and troughs – the less uniform, the better – it helps to catch the flame when you torch it. Use a blowtorch to toast the meringue until golden. Scatter with basil leaves to serve.

ⓦ **good**food

Basic sweet pastry

🕐 **1–2 hours**
Makes enough for two 28cm round pie bases and lids

This dough is very short with a high butter to flour ratio. It holds its shape and is perfect for holding pie filling. It can be kept overnight in the fridge and also freezes well. This recipe makes enough for two pie bases and two lids.

500g unsalted butter, softened but still cold
50g icing sugar, sifted
200g caster sugar
2 tsp salt
5 egg yolks
660g plain flour

1. Put the butter, icing sugar, caster sugar and salt in a bowl and using a wooden spoon, mix well to combine. Add the egg yolks, 1 at a time, until incorporated. Fold through the flour until just combined. Turn out onto a clean work surface and gather together.

2. Divide the pastry into 4 portions and shape into round, flat discs. Wrap each disc in plastic wrap and refrigerate for at least 2 hours (or freeze for future use).

3. Remove the pastry disc from the fridge 20 minutes before using. Roll out the pastry between 2 sheets of baking paper until 3mm-thick. Place on trays and refrigerate again for at least 20 minutes. Use in your recipe.

Pavlova base

🕐 **1–2 hours**
Serves 6–8

Create your dream pavlova by starting with this traditional base recipe (rectangle, rather than round), then add beautiful toppings to your heart's content.

8 eggwhites, at room temperature
500g caster sugar
20g cornflour
dash white wine vinegar or lemon juice
1 vanilla bean, seeds scraped

1. Preheat oven to 130°C. Line a large baking tray (approximately. 40cm x 30cm) with baking paper.

3. Add eggwhites to a clean dry bowl of an electric mixer. Whisk on medium until you see ribbons starting to form across the top of the mixture. Very gradually begin to add the sugar, about a tablespoon at a time, so it is well incorporated into the eggwhite. Once all sugar has been added, increase mixer speed to high and whip for about 3 minutes then turn off the mixer. Gently sift over the cornflour and then add the white wine vinegar and vanilla and stir to combine.

4. Turn out onto prepared tray and, using a palette knife or spatula, spread the mixture across the baking paper, creating a few tips and dips in the meringue as you go.

5. Place in the oven and immediately turn oven down to 100°C. Bake for 45 minutes–1 hour then turn off the oven and leave the pavlova to finish cooking. Don't rush this component, leave it for at least 2 hours to ensure it has time to set and forms a lovely thick crust.

goodfood

KATRINA MEYNINK

Pavlova with grilled peaches and tahini caramel

① 1–2 hours
Serves 6–8

Garnish your pavlova with grilled peaches and tahini caramel for a Middle Eastern twist.

3 peaches, halved, stone removed, cut into wedges
1 tbsp brown sugar
2 cups creme fraiche
2 tsp ground cardamom
1 tbsp vanilla paste or seeds of 2 vanilla beans, scraped
1 pavlova base (see recipe, left)
candied orange slices (optional)
¼ cup almonds, roughly chopped and lightly toasted

Tahini caramel
200g caster sugar
120ml water
100g salted butter, cubed
100ml cream
150g tahini paste

1. To make the caramel, put the sugar and water in a saucepan and place over low-medium heat. Stir occasionally until the sugar dissolves then increase the heat to high and cook until the sugar is a lovely brown hue. Remove from heat and add the butter and cream, be careful as mixture will spit. Whisk constantly to prevent any seizing. Add the tahini and any extra salt to taste. Set aside to cool slightly.

2. For the peaches, heat a barbecue or char grill pan to medium. Lightly toss peaches in brown sugar to roughly coat and grill until charred (1-2 minutes each side). Transfer to a plate to cool.

3. Combine the creme fraiche, cardamom and vanilla in a bowl then top meringue base with dollops of the creme fraiche mixture. Top with grilled peaches, candied orange slices and toasted almonds. Drizzle over tahini caramel and serve immediately with extra tahini caramel.

goodfood

Chocolate, coconut butterscotch and raspberry trifle

🕐 **2 hours +**
Serves 8–10

It's custard, it's cake, it's fruit, it's booze – what's not to like? It's true, this is not a purist's recipe. I have taken a bit of creative licence but hopefully you can find room in your hearts for this version. It's a few steps, but you don't have to conquer it all in one day. You can almost fully assemble it the day ahead, leaving only the last step of adding whipped cream and final topping just before serving. It's worth making your own genoise – although store-bought sponge will save time, the results will not be as good.

Chocolate genoise sponge
100g plain flour
35g cocoa powder
1 tsp baking powder
¼ tsp salt
3 eggs, at room temperature
3 egg yolks, at room temperature
170g sugar
1 tsp vanilla extract
30g butter
60ml milk

Coconut butterscotch custard
60g butter
190g dark brown sugar
60g cornflour
800ml coconut milk (two cans, preferably organic and free of additives)
200ml milk
1 tsp salt
20ml vanilla extract

Chocolate genoise sponge

1. Line the base of a greased 23cm round cake tin with baking paper. Preheat oven to 175°C.

2. Sift flour, cocoa, baking powder and salt together. Whip eggs, yolks and sugar on high in the bowl of a stand mixer until ribbons form and the volume has nearly tripled. Add vanilla when nearly there.

3. Heat the milk and butter until hot but not boiling and set aside. In 3 batches, fold the sifted dry ingredients into the egg mixture by hand, using a spatula and holding the bowl at an angle towards you. Gently fold from the centre of the bowl down to the base and scrape from the edge to the top of the bowl and back to the centre. Repeat this a few times until the dry ingredients are mixing in and there are no pockets of flour.

4. After the second batch, add a bit of the hot milk and butter mix and fold in. This activates the baking powder so the mix will puff up again. Then fold in the last of the dry ingredients and the remaining milk mixture. Fold again and immediately pour into prepared tin.

5. Bake for 30 minutes until puffed and springy when touched. Allow to cool in the tin and then flip it out. You should be able to slice this cake into 3 thin rounds. If you prefer to do two layers only, slice it in half horizontally.

Coconut butterscotch custard

1. Melt butter and sugar together over medium-high heat in a large heavy-based saucepan and let sugar melt and the colour deepen. This takes about 10 minutes. Add the cornflour and whisk in until completely smooth. Then, slowly and carefully pour the coconut milk and milk in a steady stream into the saucepan while continuously whisking. At this point also add the salt and vanilla. Switch to a spatula and keep stirring until it just simmers and the custard has thickened.

Recipe continues >

Desserts and treats

Raspberry prosecco jelly

1kg raspberries (fresh or frozen)

1 litre water

700g sugar

juice of 1 lemon

100ml prosecco

5 sheets titanium-strength
  gelatin sheets

Pedro Ximenez caramel sauce

200g brown sugar

55g butter

100ml cream

pinch of salt

60ml Pedro Ximenez sweet sherry

To assemble

extra pedro ximenez sweet sherry

150ml cream

125g fresh raspberries

100g toasted coconut chips
  (or flakes)

2. Strain through a fine sieve and allow to cool slightly. If you are not using straight away, press a layer of high-density freezer film (such as Glad Go-Between) on top of the pudding so a skin does not form on top. You'll want to pour this over the genoise while the cake is still slightly warm so that more is absorbed.

Raspberry and prosecco jelly

1. Combine berries, water, sugar and lemon in a pot and bring to a simmer. Simmer for 8-10 minutes until raspberries are broken down. Remove from heat and allow to cool in the fridge.

2. Pass this mix through a fine sieve to remove the seeds, then add the prosecco. In a small bowl, bloom your gelatin sheets in cold water until they are soft and pliable then remove from the water. Squeeze out the excess liquid and put the sheets in a small pot with half a cup of the raspberry liquid. Gently warm this mix to just dissolve the gelatin. Be careful not to heat it too much or the gelatin will deactivate. Immediately stir this into the rest of the raspberry mix, pour into a large container and refrigerate overnight to set.

Pedro Ximenez caramel sauce

1. Mix sugar and butter together in a saucepan over medium heat and cook until sugar has melted and the colour is beginning to deepen and caramelise further.

2. Remove from the heat and add the cream, salt and sherry. Take care as the mixture may spatter. Stir to combine. Refrigerate overnight. The next day, warm gently so it becomes more pourable.

To assemble

1. The day before serving, slice the cake in three layers (if you haven't already) and trim them to fit in a large trifle bowl. Gently warm the custard.

2. Place a layer of cake down first. Then splash it really well with sherry (how much depends on how you like it but this sponge can take more than you think). Top that with a drizzle of the caramel sauce and half of the warm custard. (Doing this while warm will allow more of the custard to soak into the cake.) Let this cool for about 10 minutes before roughly breaking up the jelly and adding half to avoid melting the jelly.

3. Repeat this process with the next layer, starting with the cake, and finishing with the third cake layer and a splash of sherry. Keep a little of the pedro ximenez caramel sauce aside for final assembly. Do not add anything else to the last cake layer. At this stage, cover the trifle and put it in the fridge overnight.

To serve

Whip the cream until soft peaks form and spread on top of the cake. Top with raspberries, toasted coconut chips and a final drizzle of caramel.

good*food*

Chocolate mousse

Easy
Nut-free
Gluten-free
🕒 **less than 30 mins**
Serves 4

125g dark chocolate
   (gluten-free if required)
50g unsalted butter
150ml cream
2 egg yolks
3 eggwhites
45g caster sugar

This classic dessert is a stalwart of dinner parties and delicious crowdpleaser. It is super simple to make and is beautiful served with fresh raspberries.

1. Chop the chocolate into pieces and melt over a double-boiler. Add the butter, stir until smooth. Set aside to cool.

2. Whip the cream to stiff peaks. Beat the egg yolks and blend into the cream. Whisk the eggwhites until frothy, then, while still whisking, add a third of the sugar a little at a time until the eggwhites are smooth and shiny. Gradually add the remaining sugar, whisking until stiff peaks form.

3. Carefully fold the eggwhites into the cream mixture, one third at a time. Fold in the melted chocolate mixture, making sure it is thoroughly incorporated. Spoon the mix into 4 cups or glasses and refrigerate for at least 3 hours.

4. Whip some additional cream and place a dollop on top of the mousse. You can also grate chocolate over the cream, a classic way to finish a classic dessert.

Desserts and treats

Secret ingredient chewy choc-chip cookies

Easy
⏱ **Less than 30 mins**
Makes 25

180g unsalted butter, melted
180g white or unrefined sugar
80g dark brown sugar
1 egg (60g)
30ml beer, cola or orange juice
2 tsp vanilla extract
330g plain flour
¼ tsp bicarbonate of soda
200g milk or dark chocolate,
   chopped in small cubes

Supremely dense, soft thick biscuits. The craft beer adds an utterly subtle spiced hint, better with it for me, though you can replace it with any other drink like cola for a curious background flavour that will have everyone guessing.

1. Put the melted butter, white and brown sugars, egg, cola and vanilla in a bowl and beat until the sugar is dissolved and the mixture is smooth and satiny.

2. Add the flour and bicarb, beat until smooth, then mix in three-quarters of the chocolate cubes evenly. Chill mixture until firm.

3. Weigh into 40g pieces, roll into balls between your hands and press flat-ish onto the tray: they don't spread much. Press the remaining chocolate chips into the tops of the cookies.

4. Bake at 160°C (140°C fan-forced) for about 15 minutes until lightly golden but still slightly undercooked and soft in the middle.

Chocolate carrot brownie bar

Easy
🕐 **45 minutes**
Serves 4–6

Now here's an exciting new twist on chocolate brownies. The mixture of milk and dark chocolate is a nifty trick from Tasmanian chef Alistair Wise from Sweet Envy in Hobart, that gives the best marriage of milk chocolate's comfort and creaminess, and dark chocolate's cocoa intensity.

Melted butter, for greasing
80g unsalted butter, softened
160g caster sugar
1 egg, plus one extra yolk
100g milk chocolate
100g dark chocolate
   (70 per cent cocoa)
40ml hot espresso-strength coffee
10ml brandy or milk
50g finely grated carrot
110g plain white flour, plus extra
   for dusting
½ tsp baking powder
11 macadamia nuts, shelled

1. Brush the inside of a 25cm x 10cm fluted tart tin with melted butter and dust evenly with flour.

2. Using electric beaters, whisk butter and sugar until smooth and light, then whisk in the egg and yolk on high speed until light and pale.

3. Melt the chocolates together, stir them through the butter mixture evenly with the coffee and brandy.

4. Stir in the carrot, flour and baking powder then spoon into the prepared tin evenly. Dot with the macadamia nuts, then bake at 160°C fan-forced for 25 minutes. Cool before cutting into slices.

Index

Index